VALUE

SOURCING

The Future of IT Outsourcing

VALUE

SOURCING

The Future of IT Outsourcing

ALOK KUMAR
KEITH SHERWELL

Declaration

Authors have attempted to put their experience of several decades in technology, outsourcing and offshoring to take the reader through a journey of the IT outsourcing over several decades and even relating the same to historical facts to establish the future of outsourcing and the way outsourcing would be done. They have coined the word "Value Sourcing" to refer to the outcome based outsourcing which constantly adds value to the end customer experience which they practice extensively within their organization.

This book is written with USA and India, the two IT giants as primary focus and intended for CXOs, senior management, planners and IT professionals of any function who are involved in creating strategy and planning for a better outcome from their current outsourcing.

PREFACE

History has shown several times and established the fact that the underlying factor for outsourcing is to lower cost and provide better value of the services and goods to the buyers to what they can achieve themselves. There can be reasons of outsourcing done by organizations at a higher cost than what they themselves can achieve, however this will always remain a temporary form of outsourcing because the buyer will eventually either develop the skill in-house or find a better source which can give him cost advantage and higher value.

Any service which was cost effective earlier but loses its cost advantage due to whatever reason gives way to another form of service which can do this task at a lower overall cost and higher value to the end consumer, thereby re-establishing the low cost and high value basis of outsourcing.

More than two decades back, when outsourcing in manufacturing was highly established, it was difficult to understand how we could outsource anything that cannot be seen, checked and counted. Manufacturing was all about the physical piece being counted and checked and was very straightforward. Once I visited a vendor myself in Chennai who was making pins and brushes for the trucks my company was producing. These items were small and insignificant in nature as compared to the overall cost of the vehicle. The same component when imported was costing almost double to the cost of local manufacture by this vendor. In my discussion with the vendor, I figured out that the vendor was saving almost fifty percent of the cost he was billing us. I came back to my manager and asked him the reason for this outsourcing when we could save yet another fifty percent of the cost. He replied back that it was value sourcing and not outsourcing. My company would end up spending more on the manufacture of the component as much more higher value added work needs focus than these small ones. He also pointed out that the vendor I met did not have such a large complex, so many high paid managers nor such great office space too. These overheads which were not with the vendor helped him save this money for himself and even helped us to save money on the imported component.

Since then, I always looked at outsourcing as value sourcing and questioned the validity of the outsourcing if it failed to generate the desired value. I moved from manufacturing to services and saw the outsourcing model between USA and Indian IT companies mature. Two decades back, it was only cost arbitrage that made this model work. Skills were very basic and engineers learned on the job.

Over period of next two decades, the demand matured to higher skills and experience than just bodies. We clearly see that the paradigm of value have been shifting in IT outsourcing and the definition of value is no more just cost but an outcome which will help the customer provide better value to their end customer.

We discovered that although claimed by several outsourcing companies, most of them still are struggling to change themselves into a true value source. Keith and I are working to get true value sourcing with the

partners and helping this to generate an outcome, which will provide higher value of our goods and services to our end customer.

We acknowledge the hard and dedicated work of Tavisha Tandon who helped us complete this book. Our colleagues of Sears India have been very helpful in giving their feedback and views and their practical experience in value sourcing.

ALOK KUMAR

Alok Kumar is a seasoned IT management professional, focused on bringing stakeholder value through innovation and creating value in challenging environments. He has a strong background in manufacturing, telecom and retail domains.

 Alok has been responsible for setting up Sears Holdings India offshore development center. In a very short span of time, he has build a capable team generating very high value for Sears. Alok is working closely with Sears Holdings executive team to chart out future value generating strategies and executing them with perfection. The best practices in Sears India have resulted in propelling Sears India up the value chain. It has been rated as the Golden Company for the year 2011 by the Economic Times of India.

Prior to Sears, Alok was SVP and headed technology program management practice for Reliance Industries in India. He was instrumental in creating Reliance Infosolutions, the captive IT unit of Reliance and was part of the core team which started Reliance Retail. He established several best practices including creating a program management tool which was awarded as the best project by Data Quest and PC Quest. Alok has received several awards in his four-year tenure with Reliance. He was awarded "CIO - Ones to Watch" award in 2008 recognizing him amongst top twenty IT executives as hot contenders for CIO positions in India. in 2013, Alok was awarded the "Emerging Leader of the year" in IT sector in India by the India Greatest forum.

Prior to Reliance, Alok held positions of CIO level with three companies with an impregnable track record of achievements all along.

Alok has published "Handwriting Speaks" in 2005, which is a book on graphology. He writes on management subjects on his blog and is a regular speaker to various forums and management institutes.

KEITH SHERWELL

A seasoned IT executive and strong leader, focused on creating business value with emphasis on delivery of quality services and achievement of results, with a strong background in large financial organizations.

 In his career, Keith has been a catalyst for innovation and change as a transformational leader. At Sears he worked to increase business value through the development and implementation of a radical transformation strategy encompassing all aspects of Technology, Service Development, Delivery and Maintenance. He believes in running IT as a business to bring out best out of in-house technology teams. Creating a strong business focused organizational design, and appropriate talent mix to capitalize on a blend of onshore/offshore associates have been key achievements of Keith.

Formally, Keith was SVP at American Express where he lead the re-architecture of the company's Global Network Infrastructure and associated transformation of the company's Network Operations and Site Services functions. Prior to that, as Business Group CIO, he led the technology strategy, delivery and operation for the International Consumer, Business Operations, Global Corporate Services and the American Express Bank. In this role he also lead a multiyear program to replace the companies disparate Card Processing systems (16) with a single Global system supporting over 22 markets whilst transforming the company's ability to launch products quickly and at a fraction of the previous costs.

Before moving to the United States he held various Senior Delivery and Operational roles in the United Kingdom with National Westminster Bank and Grand Metropolitan.

CONTENTS

INTRODUCTION

The concept of contracting a function or process by a company to an outside entity by purchasing it as a service and ceasing to perform that function or process internally, is what can be broadly referred to as outsourcing. It is usually in terms of procuring business related functions and services, for example the outsourcing of IT. Since the 1970s, IT outsourcing has become a top priority of numerous companies belonging to varied fields. What started from outsourcing a single task has moved on to outsourcing complex processes, considerably changing the whole structure of industries. The term outsourcing is an artificial construction composed of the words "outside", "resource" and "using". Outsourcing involves the transfer of tasks and services, previously performed in-house, to external vendors. Similarly, IT outsourcing involves turning over various IT activities to external vendors. It is thus linked to the traditional make-or-buy problem, i.e. the decision whether to purchase goods or services available in the market or to provide for them internally. Companies since the past have always hired contractors for particular types of work, or to level-off peaks and troughs in their workload. Long-term relationships have been formed in the past with vendors whose capabilities supplemented that of their own company. However, the core difference between simply supplementing capabilities by subcontracting and actual outsourcing is that outsourcing involves a substantial restructuring of particular business activities including the transfer of staff from a host company to a specialist company with the required core competencies. Outsourcing externalizes activities, leading to a reduction of a company's value chain activities and paving the way to a streamlined organizational structure. There is also an increase in the division of labor within and sometimes across economies.

In 2001, the People's Republic to China, after the accession to the World Trade Organization, emerged as a prominent destination for offshoring of production, especially of apparels, toys, and consumer goods. Also known as physical restructuring, production offshoring got its big push when the North American Free Trade Agreement (NAFTA) made it easier for manufacturers to shift production facilities from the US to Mexico. This trend then shifted to China, which offered cheap prices through very low wages, few workers' rights laws, a fixed currency pegged to the US dollar, cheap loans, land and factories for new companies, few environmental regulations, and huge economies of scale in cities with population over a million workers dedicated to producing a single kind of product. However, only the manufacturing of products were shipped out and the design, research and development process of new products remained within the home nations as it required a skill set that was harder to obtain in regions with cheap labor.

Following the telecommunication and Internet expansion in the late 1990s along with digitalization of various services, reliable and affordable communication infrastructure developed. This in turn led to the growth and outsourcing of IT-enabled services such as finance and accounting, HR, legal, call centres, marketing and sales services, IT infrastructure, application development, knowledge services including engineering support, product design, research and development, and analytics.

India fitted the bill perfectly for outsourcing because of a large pool of English speaking population and technically proficient manpower. India's outsourcing industry took root in low-end IT functions in the early 1990s and moved on to back-office processes such as call centers and transaction processing. In the late 1990s, India's abundant and well qualified software engineering talent combined with massive demand from the Y2K problem helped India attract large-scale software development projects from US and Europe based customers. Currently, India's engineering talent has presence in various outsourcing destinations and in various global firms like HP, IBM, Accenture, Intel, AMD, Microsoft, Oracle Corporation, Cisco, SAP, and BEA. Indian IT sector has witnessed a 10 - 15% wage growth in the 21st century! Interestingly, the choice of outsourcing destination is usually made according to cultural concerns, especially the language spoken. For example, Japanese companies are outsourcing to China, where large numbers of Japanese speakers can be found. German companies tend to outsource to Poland and Romania, where proficiency in German is common. French companies outsource to North Africa for similar reasons. For Australian IT companies, Indonesia is one of the major choice of outsourcing destination. Other outsourcing destinations include Mexico, Central and South America, the Philippines, South Africa and Eastern European countries. Access to lower cost economies offers a great cost saving option. The labor arbitrage generated by the wage gap between industrialized and developing nations greatly helps lowering the overall cost of the service. Then resources of the company in terms of investment, people and infrastructure can be focused on developing the core business. And that is why many companies outsource their IT support to specialized IT services companies, which also helps in improving the quality of the service. The outsourced service is viewed with wider experience and knowledge and opportunity for best operational practices that would otherwise be too difficult, expensive or time consuming to develop in-house. A large talent pool and skills of various degrees, particularly in science and engineering, which exist outside the origin country can be tapped into for further augmentation of the service. It also serves as a good catalyst for change with the outsourcer becoming a change agent in the process. Moreover, external knowledge service providers supplement to the limited in-house capacity for product innovation. Tax benefit and easy scalability options further add to the many positives of outsourcing.

IT outsourcing is heterogeneous and can take various forms, depending on various factors. External domestic IT outsourcing can be regarded as the origin of IT outsourcing. In this, companies engage in an outsourcing relationship with a domestic IT provider. For example, in 1989 Eastman Kodak's decision to outsource its information technology systems to IBM was considered revolutionary. They were quickly followed by dozens of major corporations whose managers had determined that it was not necessary to own the technology to get access to the information they needed. The recent

trend is of outsourcing IT externally across

international borders. Today, companies are no longer restricted to domestic IT outsourcing providers. The Internet boom and low cost communication has provided the basis for transferring certain IT activities to almost any place on the globe. Now, many companies have international IT outsourcing contracts with IT providers located thousands of miles away. Sometimes, IT activities are not externalized but stay within the local organization known as internal domestic IT provision. And there are captive units, which usually take the form of subsidiaries or joint ventures abroad, for example, the IT offshore subsidiaries of SAP or Siemens in Bangalore/ India. Such company owned

off-shore international operations are also termed as GIC or Global in-house centers.

Today outsourcing affects nearly all functions of an organization. It has become rather a cross-functional activity. Outsourcing is applied to satisfy the organization's hardware and software needs. In earlier periods, cost reduction or worker reduction were the most common reasons to outsource. However, today the reasons that drive outsourcing are more strategic such as to reduce and control the overall operating cost of the company by allocating resources in a cost saving manner to external service providers, especially in nations with cheap manpower available, thereby freeing internal resources for other purposes. Outsourcing functions that are time consuming or more expensive to perform in-house can be outsourced to ensure a much more concerted effort, leading to faster output and helping bring to focus the primary objective of the host company. Outsourcing also provides a good option for companies with insufficient resources available to meet the cost of an operation. Besides, companies get access to world-class capabilities, which may be unavailable in-house, and share the risk of the venture with their partner companies.

Most outsourcing takes place in financial services, which has the largest IT budget of all industries, followed by manufacturing and governmental institutions. Financial services industries have heavily IT dependent processes and so by strategically outsourcing part of these processes, they are able to achieve cost savings of almost 8% to 12%. This industry is also a pioneer in IT outsourcing strategies such as IT offshoring, which is more lucrative, though also more risky, but it most definitely offers them even greater cost reduction.

Besides cost saving, there are many other forces – or "drivers" that lead to outsourcing by companies. Companies reshape their current organizational structure by outsourcing. In the context of IT, it can be pointed out that the life cycles of most hardware and software products have drastically decreased due to rapid innovations. This has resulted in intense competition in the IT industry, and this rivalry is further spurred through forces of globalization. As a result, various researchers regard globalization as one major driver for outsourcing. Many believe focusing on core competencies as a primary outsourcing driver, allowing companies undistracted focus on key priorities, or re-focusing on those areas where business opportunities can be achieved. Another reason for IT outsourcing is to reach sufficient economies of scale. Economies of scale can be reached on the supplier's side, for instance, as a large number of computer manufacturers outsource assembly to one supplier. The supplier is then able to work on full capacity and thus save costs, which can be passed back to the buyer in the form of lower prices. Buyers can experience the same cost reduction results if they solely focus on specific operations and outsource those whose capacity is too small. Besides, there are other reasons for outsourcing such as scarcity of capital, lack of know-how, increase flexibility, save on time to market, and optimal asset utilization.

TOP 10 REASONS COMPANIES OUTSOURCE

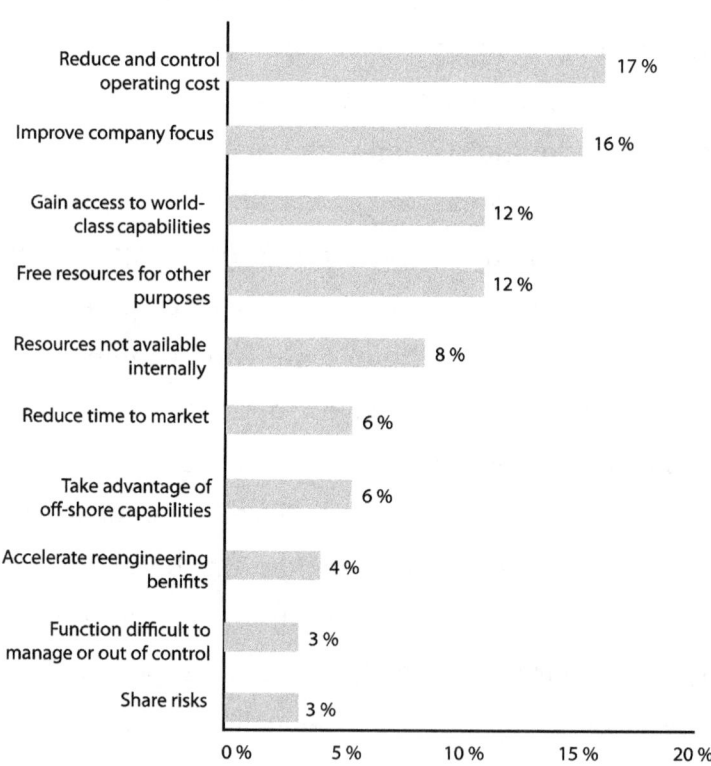

O N E

OTHER FORMS
OF OUTSOURCING

Initially, people moved to the place of work. With advancement in transportation, large scale colonization started with offshoring the work partially. Modern economies and telecom revolution has enabled work to move freely between geographical boundaries without displacing people.

Outsourcing of labor and work is not just a feature of the new world, but a method that existed hundreds of years ago for the same reasons why it exists today, and that is to save cost in terms of cheap labor and lack of skilled labor within a home country. Today, the IT outsourcing serves as a cost-effective way for companies to hire qualified individuals for specific IT jobs at a significantly lower cost and without committing to the costs of maintaining in-house teams. Outsourcing many years ago, whether it was human or service, too served as a cost cutting venture. It ranged from a scale of states within a country to even nations that were oceans apart. In the earlier years, telecommunication and Internet did not exist and there was not much of technological advancement. Economies were mostly agricultural and labor needs were mainly to support the agricultural industry. Shortage of labor led to transportation of labor from other nations where cheap labor was available. The demand was mostly for unskilled labor to work in farms and plantations. Labor migration also led to migration of families to new locations and many later became permanent settlers there.

OUTSOURCING OF CHEAP LABOR

Slaves in US served labor needs

In the 17th century, nearly two-thirds of English settlers came as indentured servants to colonial America. Farmers, planters and shopkeepers in colonial North America found it difficult to hire free labor. There was shortage of money and native work force was sparse. It was not easy for a farmer to manage his own farm. This led to the growth of indentured labors who were mostly white immigrants, which included Scots, Irish and Germans. Thus, indenturing servants severed as a way for outsourcing the work to outsiders for the reason of cheap, skilled labor. Only at that time, they were brought to the host country. With time, indenturing servants was becoming difficult. An improving economy in England in the late 17th century and early 18th century led to fewer workers wanting to go to the colonies in search of work. They would rather find work in their native lands. There was also a problem of high mortality rate among the indentured servants. This lead to a gradual transformation of the status of indentured servants to slaves, whereby they were bound for life to work as servants and could never leave. By 1750, Georgia authorized slavery as they were unable to acquire enough indentured servants. Soon, slavery existed in all colonies. In the north, salves were used as house servants, artisans, laborers and craftsmen, whereas in the South, they were mainly used as laborers in agricultural lands. The population of slaves in the South was higher than that in the North, as the South was solely an agricultural economy and its commodity crops were labor intensive. Slaves worked on farms and plantations to grow rice, indigo, tobacco and cotton. In 1793, the cotton gin was invented which made processing of short-staple cotton economical. There was an explosive growth of cotton cultivation throughout the Deep South, with many plantation owners moving further west in search of suitable land. This was followed by an increasing demand for slave labor to support the mass expansion of cotton plantation in the Deep South. The boom in agricultural economies in the Deep South resulted in forced migration of slaves westward and southward. The internal slave trade became a major economic activity by 1815. Between 1830 and 1840, nearly 250000 slaves were displaced and moved to the South.

The first half the 19th century saw many abolitionist movements take place throughout the US. Amongst the Southerners, there was strong support for slavery as it profited them greatly. Even the banking, shipping and manufacturing industries of New York had strong economic interest in the continuation of slavery. In 1863, during the Civil War, Lincoln, using his war powers, issued an executive order known as the Emancipation Proclamation. The Emancipation Proclamation called for immediate freedom of the slaves in ten states in the South that were in rebellion during the war. In 1865, the Proclamation immediately freed 50,000 slaves; with nearly all the rest (of the 3.1 million) freed as the Union armies advanced. To completely abolish slavery, the Thirteenth Amendment was passed by the Senate in April

1864 and by the House of Representatives in January 1865. The amendment was ratified on December 6, 1865 by three fourth sates and on that day all salves became officially free.

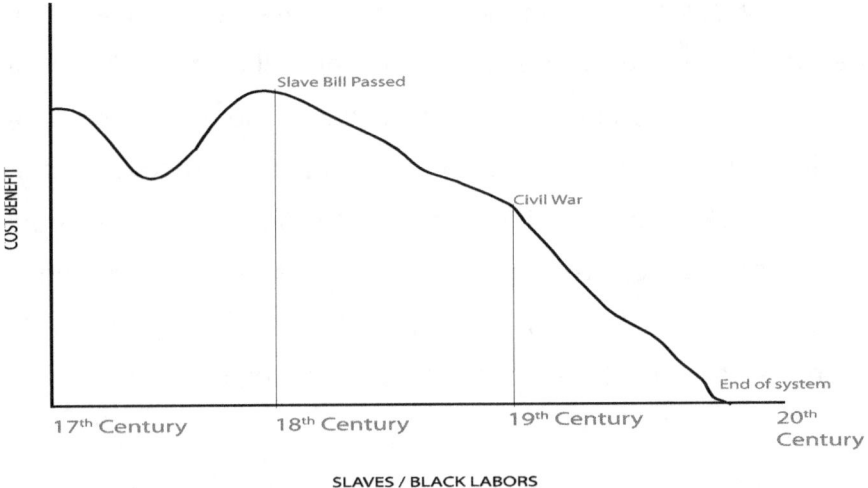

SLAVES / BLACK LABORS

Labor demand in British Colonies

The British had many colonies in the world and majority of British immigrants were from these colonies. Many even migrated after the colonies were granted independence. These immigrants were mostly from the Indian subcontinent and the Caribbean. To fill the gap in the UK labor market for unskilled jobs, the British Nationality Act 1948 was passed after World War II, allowing 0.8 million immigrants to live and work in the UK without a visa. Some of these 'economic migrants' were specially brought on ships. Over the years, as the number of commonwealth immigrants swelled drastically, a cabinet committee was established and the Commonwealth Immigration Act was passed to restrict the rising immigrants. The new act made it mandatory for migrants to have a job before they arrived or posses a special skill or meet the labor needs of the economy. Post World War II, labor demand rose as industries required labor for the economic recovery after the war. UK then recruited displaced groups of people from Soviet controlled territories. After India gained independence in 1947, many Indians arrived in UK and found work in foundries and textile factories, shops, post offices etc.

The abolition of slavery in British colonies created a huge labor shortage. In most British colonies, the sugar plantation economy was dependent on plentiful, cheap labor force for its success and profitability. Slaves had served as the backbone of these plantation colonies. To combat the shortage of labor after the abolition of slavery, the British introduced the indentured labor system in 1835. This led to the arrival of hundreds and thousands of workers from India. Mauritius was the first British colony to import indentured labor from India, mostly from Bengal (currently Bangladesh and West Bengal province of India). Indian indentured labors were also imported in British Guiana, Trinidad, Jamaica, Ceylon and Federated Malay States and South Africa.

Fiji faced a similar problem of shortage of labor. Fiji, which was under the British colonial rule, required labor for work in sugarcane plantations. The British had established the sugarcane industry in Fiji to promote a stable economic base, but were unwilling to exploit indigenous labor and threaten the Fijian way of life. So the need for labor arose, which led to importation of labor from India under the indentured labor system.

The indentured Indian servants in British colonies worked on sugarcane plantations often under degrading conditions. As a result the system was abolished in 1916.

Planned immigration in Australia

Build through colonialization and immigration over the last two centuries, Australia has followed a policy of planned immigration since 1947 to build its population and bring about economic growth. In 1947, Australian government encouraged large-scale immigration for strategic purposes of populating the nation as it had just narrowly escaped a Japanese invasion. The increasing population also served as labor to the new manufacturing industries. Up to 1973, Australian immigration policies focused on recruiting manual labor force. Most of these unskilled and semi-skilled laborers were employed on construction sites and factories. Besides serving the labor needs, labor influx through immigration kept the wage pressure checked and increased the competitiveness of industries.

'Guest workers' in Germany

Germany recruited many 'guest workers' especially from the Mediterranean area. Here again labor recruitment was the driving force. The 'guest worker' system recruited manual workers to work in factories and other low-skilled jobs.

COLONIAL EMPIRES

In some cases it was not possible for the work to be moved just because of the nature of work or the basic need to perform the work. Looking at history, during the age of exploration and colonialisation, to take advantage of rich resources and labor and reap benefits through establishing trade, many colonies emerged. Colonial empires utilized the labor and resources of their colonies for profitable trade or supplying raw materials for their industries. Most of the European nations attacked and ruled nations for decades or even centuries that were rich in natural resources. Cheap cost produce was shipped out to their countries to generate huge cost advantage. Thus it was a type of outsourcing where labor or work was not moved, but instead colonies were established in resource rich countries.

The British Empire was the largest empire in history with overseas colonies and trading posts established by England for over a century. The empire covered almost a quarter of the Earth's total land area. Portugal and Spain pioneered European exploration of the globe in the 15th and 16th century and established large overseas empires, generating great amount of wealth. Their success prompted England, France and the Netherlands to establish colonies and trade networks of their own in the Americas and Asia. They also cultivated tobacco and cotton, which led to an agriculture boom in British colonies and generated huge profits for the empire. They made their way to India for the sole purpose of trade. Establishing the East India Company, they colonized and ruled India for many years and exported spices, herbs, fabrics, rice, tea and opium. Africa was colonized for similar economic reasons as it offered Britain valuable raw material and an open market to enable them to get a trade surplus. The Royal African Company established a monopoly of the trade to supply slaves to the British colonies of the Caribbean. Until slavery was abolished in 1807, Britain was responsible for the transportation of 3.5 million African slaves to America. After the loss of the 13 colonies in 1783, the British government turned to the newly discovered lands of Australia. The Australian colonies provided Britain with commercial and political gains. The continent was rich in natural resources, which England wanted, and also provided a port in the East to promote trade with China.

The French colonial empire began in 1605, but unlike England's appetite for land, they were focused on developing mercantile colonies. In 1608, Samuel De Champlain founded Quebec, which become the capital of the fur-trading colony of New France. The French placed more emphasis on the fur trade rather than agricultural settlements. In 1699, they expanded their trading network in North America with the foundation of Louisiana in the basin of the Mississippi River. They also began to establish trading posts along West African coast in 1624 and in 1664, the French East India Company was established to compete for trade in the east.

In the 16th century, Spain took over large areas on mainland North and South America to create a westward route to Asia and the sought-after Spice Islands.

At the other side of the world, following the Meiji Restoration of 1868, Japan transformed from a feudal society to a modern industrial state and became known as a newly emergent power. Japan turned its attention towards Korea to protect its own interests and security and have access to Korea's coal and iron ore deposits, which would benefit Japan's growing industrial base.

The First Sino-Japanese War took place between 1894–95, in which China was defeated by Japan and was forced to cede Formosa, and to recognize the nominal independence of Korea in the Treaty of Shimonoseki. The Qing Dynasty of China was on the brink of collapse from internal revolts and foreign imperialism, while Japan had emerged as a great power.

The Second Sino-Japanese War, which was the largest Asian war in the 20th century, was fought primarily between the Republic of China and the Empire of Japan as a result of Japanese imperialist policy to dominate China politically and militarily and to secure its vast raw material reserves and other economic resources of food and labor. Although the two countries had fought intermittently since 1931, total war started began in 1937 and ended with the surrender of Japan in 1945.

OUTSOURCING OF WORK

Technological advancements, development and growth of telecommunication and Internet brought about changes in the business scenario. Nations became more interconnected and distances merged. Telecommunication and electronics revolution made it possible to cross barriers of time and distance. All these transformations let to revolutionary changes in the way work was conducted. While the level, sophistication and platform of the work changed, it also became portable. Work could be moved from one place to another at very reasonable cost and minimum of time. Since now, the work started moving from one place to another, labor, which moved prior to such technological advancements, became more static. Thus now a labor in India could perform a work for a US company. The US company would continue to get the same advantage through outsourcing of work, i.e. cost saving and better value.

New technologies led to re-engineering in all sectors such as financial institutes, manufacturing, retail, service and government to deploy enhanced technology to reduce cost and increase competitiveness by fast communications. This gave rise to IT services and business process outsourcing. Late 1990s saw a wave of IT and BPO due to the 'dot com' boom and Y2K crisis, which caused a skilled labor shortage in the US. There was a surge in demand for computer coders, testers, software programmers, who were not available in the US but were in abundance in India. Thus India emerged as a frontrunner for US companies to meet this challenge. Many Indian companies landed with outsourcing contracts and US companies began to outsource their IT enabled business services. India offered a significant cost advantage as labor cost differentials allowed US companies to save 30-70 percent on labor cost. Over the years, India has established itself as a important country for US outsourcing.

Similar cost advantage is gained by Japan, which outsources its software trade to China. China has become Japan's biggest software outsourcing base. Dalian, which was a Japanese colony for 40 years before the end of World War II, has become the outsourcing center for IT to Japan due to its geographical proximity and availability of skilled labor force. Dalian Hi-Think Computer Technologies (DHC) Co. Ltd, one of China's leading software outsourcing firms, started outsourcing computer software from Japan in 1996. DHC's business with Japan has grown 30 percent annually since 1996.

The proximity of Bali to Australia led to Indonesia becoming an outsourcing destination to Australia. Indonesia had the advantage of being in the same time zone as Australia, and proximity made it easy for Australian IT management to travel to Bali.

While India is a leader in terms of industry size, countries such as Thailand and Indonesia are continuing to improve as popular outsourcing destinations.

Outsourcing has always taken place out of the need for cost saving and better value. When work could not be moved from one place to another, people were moved for supplying cheap labor for those works.

Later with technological advancements, people became static and worked moved easily from nations with high cost labor to nations with low cost labor. Outsourcing is not restricted to conventional things only. Outsourcing extends to military services, outsourcing of education services, legal outsourcing, medical outsourcing, etc. The purpose again is to save cost, attain flexibility and ultimately get better value.

Outsourcing of military services

Outsourcing of military services is common in the history of war. In the ancient and medieval times, governments hired mercenaries such as the Greek and Nubian men fought for the Egyptians, mercenaries took Jerusalem from the Roman Empire during the Sixth Crusade, and the British hired Hessian forces during the American Revolution. Since conscription at that time was rare, employing private militaries was the only mechanism for marshaling fighting forces. It was only after the industrial revolution and the advancements in military technology that states began to conscript and maintain standing armies for protecting national interest. However, over the years, subcontracting to Private Military companies has also increased.

PMCs offer battlefield services for hire. They are equipped with uniformed military ranks, doctrine and discipline and are capable of providing companies of commandos and battalions on short notice. Private military corporations such as Xe, Sandline and Military Professional Resources Inc. (MPRI) subcontract field services to many different types of organizations, and particularly to sovereign military agencies such as the US Army and the UK Ministry of Defense.

Before WWII, the primary role of private contractors such as Booz Allen Hamilton and Vinnell Corporation was to provide logistical support such as transportation, medical services and provisioning. Increasing technical complexity of military equipment and hardware during the Cold War led the military to rely on contractors such as DynCorp, Northup Grumman, and SAIC as technical specialists working side-by-side with deployed military personnel. However, during the Cold War, the level of co-specialization of PMCs with the organizations they served was substantially lower than it is today.

After the Cold War, PMCs increased the supply of equipments and trained soldiers. They utilized the large number of unemployed former military personnel and used armaments available at low prices from former Soviet Republics to build their military capabilities and resources comparable with those of advance western military forces. .

With the rise in intrastate conflicts, the demand for PMCs services subsequently expanded especially in Africa. Since developed nations were unwilling to intervene in such conflicts, and due to absence of formal and informal constraints, PMCs were able and willing to become involved directly in
the intrastate conflicts of developing nations. Thousands of unemployed soldiers signed lucrative contracts with PMCs for deployments at short notice into conflicts worldwide.

Penal Colony in Australia

After the American Revolutionary War, America refused to take British convicts. To solve the problem
of overcrowded prisons and correctional facilities, British looked at Australia to establish a new penal colony and also open a post in East for military purposes. Led by Captain Arthur Phillip, British sent the first fleet of prisoners in May 1787 to settle in Australia. The fleet reached a cove seven miles north of Botany Bay, which later became Sydney. Most of the criminals sent to the penal colony were blue-collar citizens from England and Ireland. They worked on

government projects such as construction of roads, bridges and buildings. Over the 80 years, more than 165,000 convicts were transported to Australia. The last convict to be transported to Australia arrived in 1868.

Other services outsourced

After outsourcing of business process services, educational services are being outsourced to nations where low cost, high quality 'tutors' can be hired. Colleges are hiring online "tutors" to check grammar and other English mistakes and provide feedback to students.

Against the backdrop of the economic downturn, medical outsourcing is a trend much accelerating. Many global corporations looking to slash employees' medical bills are making Thailand and India as medical refuge, and are outsourcing their employers to these countries for medical treatments. Superior care along with low costs in internationally accredited hospitals is proving a valuable alternative to expensive western medical care.

T W O

THE BEGINNING
OF OUTSOURCING

Risky political decisions in America and a sagging economy led to high cost of local production, compelling manufacturers to seek cost effective destinations outside the US. While an ever increasing competitive global scenario propelled US to open up global trade like never before. Over the years, this outsourcing extended to technology services as well giving companies huge cost savings. Thus, cost reduction always remained the prime focus for all such outsourcing actions by US companies and to an extent it was justified due to lack of skills locally available. In order to keep the cost advantage intact, these companies continued innovating new processes.

The concept of outsourcing, as we see today, is said to date

as far back as the 1800s in America's history. At that time, the need arose primarily out of a demand for expertise and accordingly, clipper ship sails were manufactured in Scotland.

Sails had to be made to exact specifications, as that was essential for long voyages, thus outsourcing its production to where its expertise existed.

The 1970s witnessed the beginning of the computer age with rapidly developing new technologies and overall computerization of processes. During this time, US did not require much offshore expertise as there sprung up several companies who could provide such services due to the advancements made in computer technologies. But on the other side of the globe, the communist Chinese government opened the gates of trade and heavily encouraged global trade. The Chinese realized how they could benefit from harnessing the concept of job outsourcing. Thousands of factories mushroomed in various regions of China employing millions of citizens. The country soon became "the world's number one factory." 1970s was also a dark year for the Americans. Their self-confidence fell to a new low with the Vietnam War and the Watergate scandal shattering their confidence in the present presidency. There were also international frustrations, including the fall of South Vietnam in 1975, the Iran hostage crisis in 1979, the Soviet intervention in Afghanistan, the growth of international terrorism, and the acceleration of the arms race. All these situations and issues raised fears over the country's ability to control international affairs. The energy crisis was at an all-time high, unemployment rose unprecedentedly, and inflation was pegged at very high values. Interest rates escalated making economic planning difficult. The Soviet economy was lagging behind under the rule of Leonid Brezhnev. It was merely surviving due to the lucrative oil exports.

Meanwhile, détente with the Soviets collapsed as the Communists made gains across the Third World. The victory in Vietnam in 1975 when North Vietnam invaded and conquered South Vietnam led to nearly a million refugees fleeing. Most of those who survived came to the US. American forces were involved only to rescue American supporters. Other communist movements, backed by Moscow or Beijing, were spreading rapidly across Africa, Southeast Asia and Latin America. The Soviet Union, however, seemed committed to the Brezhnev Doctrine, sending troops to Afghanistan in a move denounced by the Western and Muslim countries. Against this backdrop of economic stagflation and perceived American weakness against the USSR abroad, Ronald Reagan, former governor of California, won the Republican nomination in 1980 by winning most of the primaries. Reagan picked his chief primary rival, George H.W.

Bush, as the vice-presidential nominee. He relied on Jeane Kirkpatrick as his foreign policy adviser during his campaigns. Jeane Kirkpatrick focused on identifying Carter's vulnerabilities on foreign policy matters.

Reagan made promises to end the drift in post-Vietnam U.S. foreign policy and to restore the nation's military strength. He also propagated putting an end to "big government" and restoring the economic health of the nation by relying on supply-side economics.

The supply-side economists were against the welfare state built up by the Great Society. They asserted that the cause of trouble for the U.S. economy was a large part because of excessive taxation. Excessive taxation, according to them, "crowded out" money away from private investors, and thus, it was the main reason for a stifled economic growth. So they argued that the best solution was to cut taxes across the board, particularly in the upper income brackets, to encourage private investment. They also aimed to reduce government spending on welfare and social services geared toward the poorer sectors of society which had built up during the 1960s. Regan's viewpoints were reiterated especially by the citizens of the Sun belt region, mainly the Southwest,

Southeast, Florida and California. They voted for him in the 1980 presidential elections. This election was a turning point in American politics, signaling the new electoral power of the suburbs and the Sun belt. The major issues of the campaign were the economic stagflation, threats to national security, the Iranian hostage crisis, and the general malaise that indicated that the great days of America were over. This was also the beginning of a hawkish foreign policy. Carter was unable to control inflation and had failed in the rescue effort of the hostages in Tehran.

On the other hand, Reagan won a landslide victory with 489 votes in the electoral college to Carter's 49. Republicans defeated twelve Democratic senators to regain control of the Senate for the first time in 25 years. However, the critics pointed out how Reagan was insensitive to the plight of the poor, and that anyway the economic troubles of the 1970s were beyond any president's ability to control or reverse.

Reagan's approach to the presidency was somewhat of a departure from his predecessors as he delegated a great deal of work to his subordinates, letting them handle most of the government's day-to-day affairs. He promised an economic revival that would affect all sectors of the population and proposed to achieve this goal by slashing taxes and reducing the size and scope of federal programs. The critics were quick to respond that the tax cuts would in turn reduce the revenues, leading to large federal deficits, which would lead to higher interest rates, stifling all economic benefits. But Reagan and his supporters promoted the theory of supply-side economics, claiming that the tax cuts would increase revenues through economic growth. It would also allow the federal government to balance its budget.

Reagan's 1981 economic legislation was a mixture of rival programs to appeal to all his conservative constituencies. While the Monetarists were placated by tight controls of the money supply, the cold warriors won large increases in the defense budget. The wealthy taxpayers won sweeping three-year tax rate reductions on both individual and corporate taxes and the middle class saw that its pensions and entitlements would not be targeted. Regan's budget director David Stockman put Reagan's program through Congress within the administration's deadline of forty days. He advocated the same principles himself and felt that spending cuts were needed to slash expenditures across the board, with the exception of defense expenditures. Appeals from constituencies who were threatened by the loss of social services were nothing but ineffectual and the new budget cuts easily passed through the Congress. But it was as early as 1982, when Reagan's economic program became beset with difficulties. A soaring budget deficit led to extensive government borrowing. The tightening of the money supply resulted in sky high interest rates almost to the tune of 20 percent. And a more serious problem of unemployment increased manifolds in the following years. Some regions of the "Rust Belt", which included the industrial Midwest and Northeast, descended into virtual depression conditions as steel mills and other industries shut down production. Many family farms in the Midwest and elsewhere were ruined by high interest rates. Reagan then allowed the Federal Reserve to drastically reduce the money supply to cure inflation, but it resulted in the recession deepening temporarily. Soon his popularity plummeted in the worst months of the recession of 1982. During the mid-term elections, the Democrats made sweeping victory.

In 1983 to 1984, the economy showed signs of some recovery and one of the main factors was the radical drop in oil prices due to increased production levels of the mid 1980s, which ended the inflationary pressures on fuel prices. The conservative monetarist economists began pressing for a reduction of interest rates and an expansion of the money supply. They shifted the focus to the problem of unemployment and declining investments. By the middle of 1983, unemployment fell from 11 percent in 1982 to 8.2 percent. GDP also saw a growth of 3.3 percent, which was the highest since the mid-1970s. Inflation was pegged at below 5 percent.

The 1981 tax cuts, one of the largest in U.S. history, also eroded the revenue base of the federal government in the short-term. The massive increase in military spending exceeded the cuts in social spending and by the end of 1985, funding for domestic programs had been cut drastically. The federal deficit rose from $60 billion in 1980 to a peak of $220 billion in 1986 (well over 5 % of GDP). During this time, the national debt also doubled from $749 billion to $1,746 billion. This deficit was recovered mostly by borrowing from countries, as the U.S. saving rates were very low. The United States became the world's greatest debtor from being the world's greatest creditor nation and that too within a few years. This was very damaging to America's status and was also a profound shift in the postwar international financial system, which had relied on the export of U.S. capital.

Due to the deficit, the interest rates remained quite high making the government borrow a lot of money to pay its bills. This was further driving up the price of borrowing. Although the supply-siders had promised increased investment due to top-rate and corporate tax cuts, growth and investment suffered because of the high interest rates. In October 1987, a sudden and alarming stock market crash occurred. This time, however, the Federal Reserve responded by increasing the supply of money and thus averting what could have brought about another great depression.

Another alarming situation post the Reagan-era deficits was the over-valuation of the U.S. dollar. Because of a high demand for dollars that were due in large amounts to the creditors, the dollar achieved an alarming strength against other major currencies.

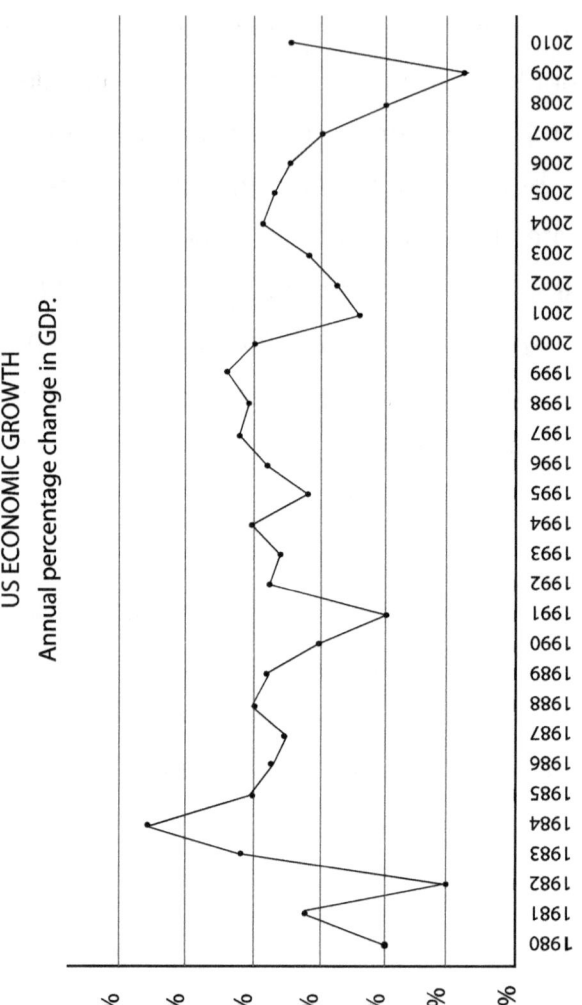

US ECONOMIC GROWTH
Annual percentage change in GDP.

source:"National Economic Accounts,"
March 2011, U.S. Bureau of Economic Analysis

As the dollar soared in value, American exports became increasingly less competitive. The high value of the dollar made it difficult for foreigners to buy American goods and encouraged Americans to buy imports. Steel and other heavy industries declined due to excessive demands by labor unions and outdated technology that made them unable to compete with Japanese imports. The consumer electronics industry was one of the worst victims of dumping and other unfair Japanese trade practices. American consumer electronics also suffered from poor quality and a relative lack of technical innovation compared to Japanese electronics. In addition, the glamorization of the financial sector including the stock market by the media and entertainment industry caused many young people to pursue careers as brokers, investors or bankers instead of manufacturing. This made it even more difficult to restore the lost industrial base. Many industrial states, including strong industrial states like Michigan and Pennsylvania suffered massive job losses. As the dollar value continued to soar to alarming numbers, some U.S. industries, especially the auto industry, clamored for immediate relief. The American government negotiated with its G-7 partners and brought down the value of the dollar.

Caught between the problems of strong dollar value and increasing foreign competition, American car companies found themselves in a desperate situation. They were forced to resort to radical measures to insure cost parity and profitability. In the mid-1980s, General Motors shut 10 factories in Flint Michigan and moved them to Mexico. The United Autoworkers Union reacted and made the transfer of jobs overseas a major issue of contention in negotiations with the big three auto manufacturers. In fact, the UAW was able to successfully negotiate agreements to prevent overseas outsourcing in the parts divisions that was spun off by GM and Ford. But by now, the U.S. companies looked at outsourcing and realized that it was a good return to profitability. This trend then began to accelerate during the 1990s. The signing of NAFTA between the United States, Mexico, and Canada made it easy for American firms to view Mexico as both a market for export and a potential center of production. Chrysler, GM and Ford expanded their Mexican production capacity and soon a host of other companies followed. Foreign owned plants staffed by Mexican labor factories called Maquiladoras sprang up everywhere along the U.S./Mexican border.

The World Trade Organization was formed at the end of WWII. Multiple rounds of trade opening simplified and lowered trade barriers. Initially, the General Agreement on Tariffs and Trade (GATT), led to a series of agreements to remove trade restrictions and then GATT's successor - the World Trade Organization (WTO) created an institution to manage the trading system. These agreements in effect made it easier for American transnational conglomerates to operate as truly global companies rather than local companies in multiple countries.

By the 1970s and 1980s, American and Japanese electronics firms such as Toshiba, Motorola, and Texas Instruments were moving more of their production facilities to low cost locations such as Taiwan and Singapore. Cost was the main motivation factor behind these relocations, which were also known as the first wave of relocations. Exports in the aftermath of the GATT and WTO doubled from 8.5% of total gross world product in 1970 to 16.2% in 2001. Many countries even shifted to bilateral or smaller multilateral agreements, such as the 2011 South Korea–United States Free Trade Agreement.

In the 1990s, the growth of low cost communication networks allowed work done using a computer to be performed without regard to location. This included accounting, software development and engineering design. The world was becoming much more interconnected and interdependent since the early 1980s. With the advent of e-mail and high-speed internet access, transnational corporations, both large and small, acquired the ability to manage and control far flung overseas divisions. U.S. multinationals were already experienced with manufacturing overseas, so they thought why not take the next logical step and begin setting up IT and research departments overseas as well. Thus began the new phase of Business Process Outsourcing. In the late 90's, this process began slowly since the economy was doing well and stock prices were up. However, the first half of 2000 saw its acceleration as the riches promised by dot com revolution evaporated into thin air. Perhaps more importantly, China and India began a concerted effort to open up their economies to the world, culminating with China's admittance to the WTO.

Many US companies saw a cost advantage in moving part of their business to such countries. Instead of hiring one engineer in the United States for $70,000, it was now possible to hire 10 engineers for the same amount of money in a developing country.

Towards the end of the 20th century, technological advancements saw the creation of self-service dashboards, which eliminated the occurrence of errors and discrepancies. As the 20th century neared to a close, the Y2K scare about the collapse of major computer systems gave rise to the need for technologies that could update computer systems in just a flash. In fact, the Y2K scare was considered as phenomenal in its effect, because it also brought the advent of the Internet. Hence, the beginning of the 21st century saw the boom in technological developments, which brought the history of outsourcing to greater heights.

Unfortunately, not enough American students were into the technological education scene at a time when technology was booming. In fact, the highest jobs in demand were for IT specialists, but only a few American candidates were considered as highly qualified. Candidates had to meet technological advancements that were becoming more and more complicated. Accordingly, during that era, there were more Asians who were pursuing science and technological courses. Only 5% of American students in the year 2001 graduated with engineering degrees and almost 60% of those who graduated with PhD degrees in Electrical Engineering were of foreign origins. An estimated 590,000 foreign students were enrolled in US colleges and universities out of which 20% were Indian and Chinese students. The proportion of their American counterpart was placed only at 5%. The number of high school seniors for 2002 who took the ACT college entrance exam to pursue degrees in engineering dwindled from 9% posted in 1992, to 6% in 2001, which further dropped only to 2% in the following year. It is said that this was because an increasing number of American students could not meet the math and science prerequisites required for the high technology subjects. Thus, education and the need for skilled labor seemed to be the foremost driving factor that led American firms to rely on the technological talents and skills of foreign service providers.

The Y2k phenomenon generated a huge demand for software engineers and programmers to fix Y2K glitches that threatened to delete vital computer data forever and disrupt flights on the eve of the millennium. Since the supply of local professionals fell short of meeting the demand, Indian talent rushed in to fill the void. Y2K opened the gates for Indian software capabilities and allowed companies like TCS and Wipro to introduce themselves to major American firms. Besides lack of skilled labor in the US, which prompted American companies to outsource parts of their work to countries that met their technical requirements, there were other factors too that contributed to boosting the outsourcing from America to other developing nations. The year 2003 was declared as the beginnings of the "Broadband Age" as telecommunication advancement continued, allowing the business sector to explore the possibilities for outsourcing other types of jobs too. The advent of high speed internet, which was now being utilized in almost every corner of the world, made it possible to share and transfer files, documents and information across the globe in seconds.

Data storage devices such as the floppy disks, magnetic tapes, punch cards, disks, flash drives and the latest cloud computing storage developed, which enhanced the possibilities of outsourcing more jobs with less of the known risks. In fact, this development in high-tech data storage has driven down the costs of manpower via outsourcing. Moreover, Internet security features also enhanced, which earlier posed a considerable threat to businesses involved with virtual transactions. New Internet security features have allowed almost all global businesses to participate virtually, to the point of eliminating physical stores and offices. Employers are in fact, hiring telecommuters to do office work.

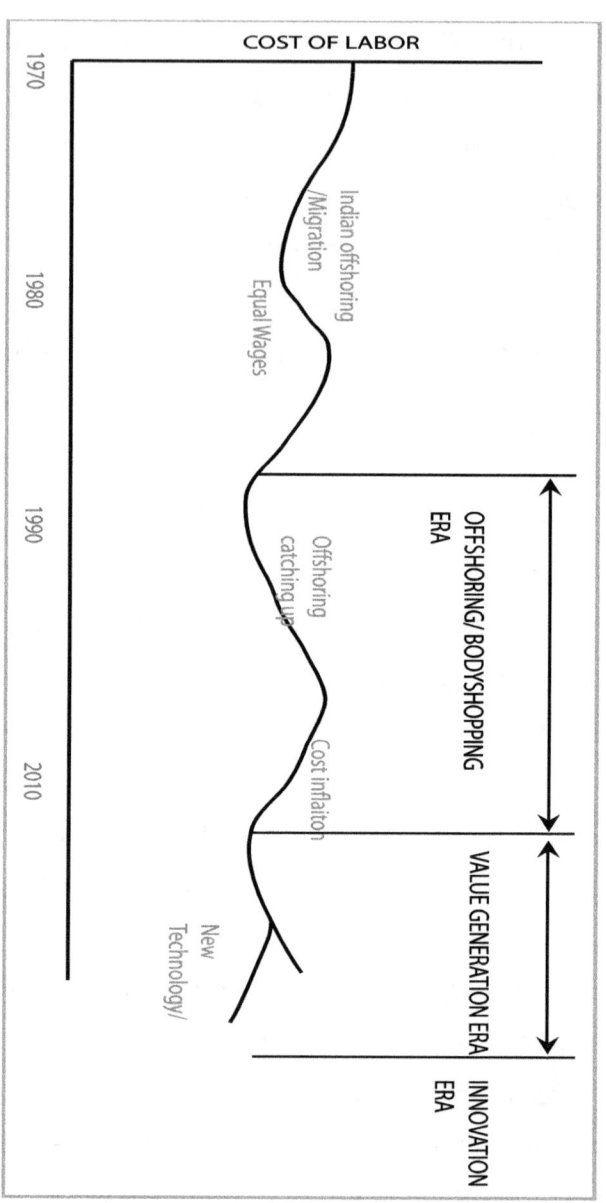

EVER EVOLVING OUTSOURCING MODEL

T W O

HISTORY OF INDIAN IT OUTSOURCING

A huge gap for IT professionals in the US due to lack of their availability locally was quickly filled in by Indian IT talent. It started with body shopping at low cost and moved on to offshoring work to reap further cost advantage. India's manpower asset along with tremendous propagation by the government and many favorable factors perfectly served the IT needs of the US and propelled India to the top of the the IT scene, second only to the US.

Growth of Information technology in India is a success story

that boasts of leading amongst developing countries. While almost two decades ago, India held an image of a country beset with poverty, unrestrained population growth and low competitiveness, today it has emerged as a rising economy with technologically skilled workforce. And this is primarily the cause of the impressive growth of the Indian software industry. Parts of India still marred with problems of infrastructure and poverty are fast receding in the background. The Indian software industry has projected a growth of more than 30 percent annually throughout the last two decades. The 1990s were the initial boom years during which software export grew to 50-60 percent annually. Even during the dot com bust, India recorded a growth of 25 percent annually, outpacing the growth in software industry anywhere in the world.

The software exports are primarily information and software services rather than products with its primary destination being the United States. India's market share of exports has rapidly grown. In terms of absolute share, its position is second only to the US. The Indian software industry is structured as a pyramid, with a few large firms dominating the sector. Amongst almost 3000 firms exporting software, the largest ones generate more than $1 billion annual sales. The smaller firms play a significant role in the domestic market, supplying software services to small and medium sized firms in different sectors.

Many of these Indian firms were started by entrepreneurs who has amassed wealth and experience in large established companies in the US, where they graduated or worked in the Silicon Valley. Thus, they were well versed in the software development processes. Moreover, high profitability and relatively low risk as compared with other industries, attracted many professionals. The cost to start a software company was not high as it did not require huge investments in land, plant or machinery and to add to the advantage, the gestation period was much shorter than in many other industries.

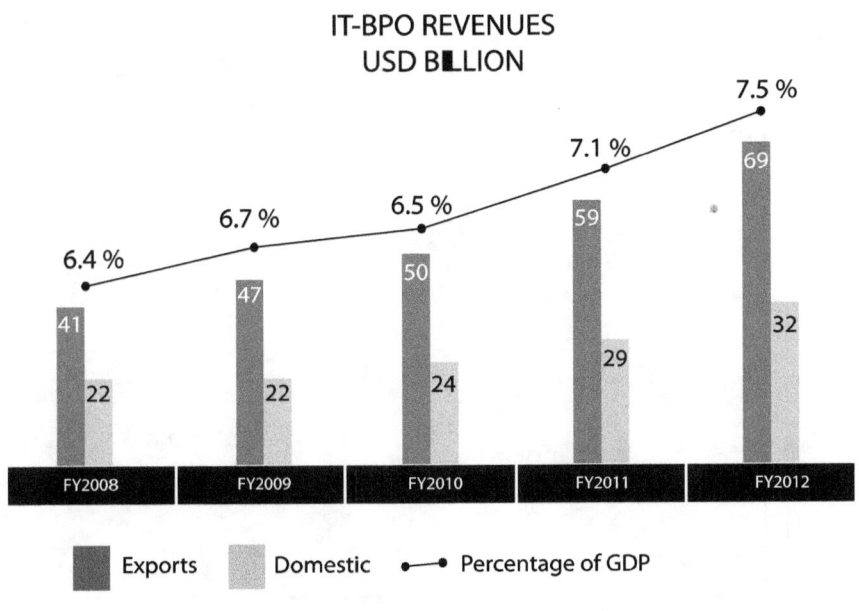

IT-BPO REVENUES
USD BILLION

Exports   Domestic   •——• Percentage of GDP

Source: NASSCOM

Today, companies from across the world are moving to India to outsource their software requirements or setting up software development centers to take advantage of the pool of talent available and recruit experienced software personnel. Over the years, India has established itself as the preferred destination for IT-BPO. There are many reasons that can be attributed to this. Globally, rapid and vast advances in technology and communication have allowed transnational companies to outsource work at a very low cost especially to countries with skilled and low cost labor.

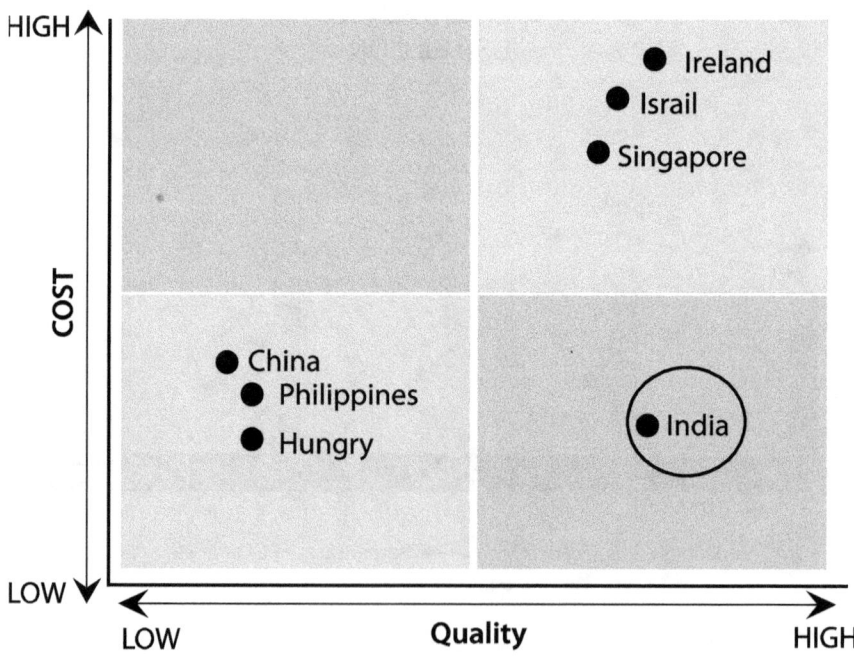

With the cost of managing workers working in a distant location drastically reduced, outsourcing became a popular option. Significantly, India also began efforts to open up its economy to the world. India has a vast pool of talent skilled in technological knowledge and with good English speaking ability. This has proved to be a major asset for the country to attract IT. Geographically, India is well located to be able to offer 24X7 service to US customers.   With the onset of globalization in the early 1990s, successive governments have pursued programs of economic reform that re-committed to maximum liberalization and privatization along with easing stringent restrictions. All this has helped the country achieve a rapid economic growth.

Developments in telephony, fibre optics and satellite communications made Internet-based communication and transfer of data possible, paving the path for outsourcing to India in a big way. The telecom industry in India used to be a controlled by the government, which held the monopoly until 1999. Thereafter, policies were introduced to reshape the structure and size of the telecom Industry and allow commercial entities to participate in almost every industry segment. The introduction of IP telephony brought about further augmentation of the telecom policies and ended the state monopoly on international calling facilities. This resulted in the cost of international connectivity declining rapidly and quality of service improving significantly, which gave a great impetus to the IT & BPO sector.

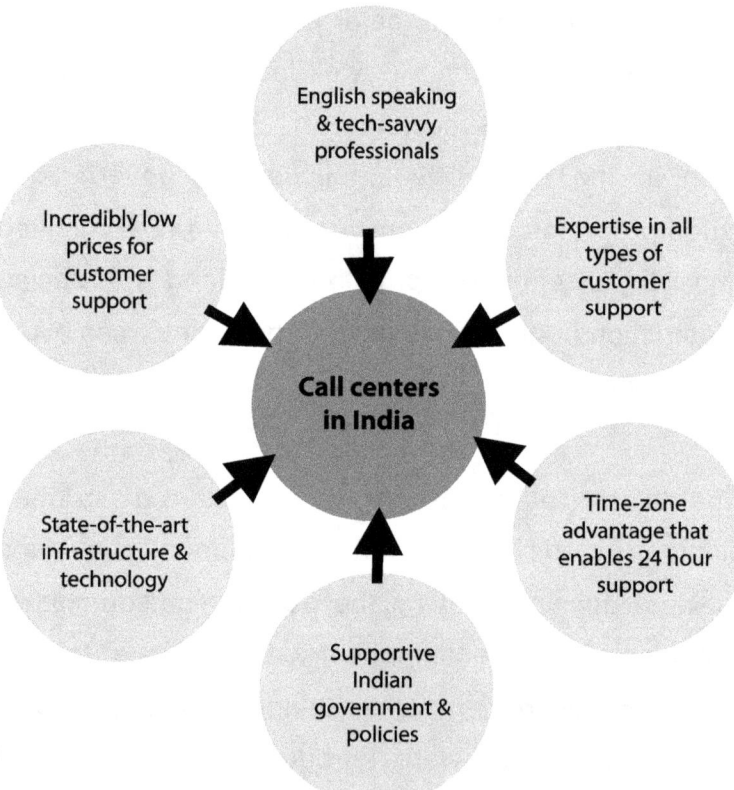

The government's liberalized investment policies resulted in several foreign companies entering Indian markets, which has been a major contributor to the growth of the Indian economy. Along with development of telecom, supporting infrastructure facilities have been constantly created and upgraded. The government has offered various tax benefits to companies and simplified stringent regulations to attract IT/BPO investment in the country. In addition to the central government's intervention, state governments are also competing with each other to offer more favorable business environments to attract IT/ITES companies to set up development units in their states. This kind of competition has greatly helped the industry grow at an astronomical rate. Over the years, global software giants like Microsoft, Oracle, SAP and many others have established captive development centers in India. On the other hand, Indian authorities have made efforts to strengthen the information security environment and have taken special initiatives to enhance the legal framework. Companies in India focus on delivering quality and performance. The internal processes and practices of many companies in India are well aligned to international standards such as ISO, CMM, Six Sigma, etc., establishing India as a credible outsourcing destination.

In a short time, India has become the largest player in offshore delivery. The levels of work delivered are amongst the highest across several verticals. India is viewed as a strategic business partner and not just an IT services vendor and many Indian companies are looking at acquisition targets worldwide. BPO too, has become the second largest segment in Indian IT/ ITES industry with Customer Care being the largest contributor. Its scope has widened over the past few years to also include KPO (Knowledge Process Outsourcing) operations. Small and Medium Providers (SMPs) in this sector are also integral to the driving force of this industry.

T W O

THE BEGINNING OF
IT IN INDIA

The Indian IT industry has existed since the early 1980s but it was only in the early '90s that saw the emergence of outsourcing. Initially, some global airlines began outsourcing their back office work to India and then IT companies followed. Some of the earliest players in the Indian outsourcing market were Texas Instruments, American Express, Swissair, British Airways and GE, who started their captive units in India.

At the time of independence in 1947, India lagged behind a great deal in terms of technological or electronics development. Years of colonial rule had led to draining of all resources of the country and the immediate needs were to cater to issues of bankruptcy. Even though Sir J.C. Bose had invented Radio Technology in 1896 (though it is believed that Marconi did so, but he was actually part of audience during a demonstration by Bose), yet at the dawn of independence there was no local manufacturing of any radio technology based equipment. It was not until 1948, when Philips set up India's first electronics manufacturing factory in Calcutta. On the other hand, telephone technology came as early as 1882 when the Oriental Telephone Company of England installed the first telephone exchanges in Calcutta, Madras and Bombay. But the equipment was brought from Bell Telephones in the USA and some from Ericsson in Sweden. It was only in 1948 when the first locally manufactured telephone exchange was set up by Indian Telephone Industries Ltd., Bangalore.

India picked up a lot of lessons from the war era developments in radar systems, microwave technology, long-range radio broadcasting, first analogue computers and innovative communication technologies. These lessons were a great impetus to subsequent developments in industry in India after independence.

As far as computers were concerned, the Indian government had been procuring EVS EM computers from the Soviet Union. They were used in large companies and research laboratories. Post-independence political and economic agenda focused heavily on making the country self-sufficient in terms of electronics and technology. The main aim was to reduce the dependence on foreign technology and instead produce its own technology and achieve indigenization of technology. Self-sufficiency in computers and electronics was also motivated by national security concerns relates to border conflicts with China and Pakistan. For these purposes, the government set up the Electronics Committee to respond to the perceived security issue and cater to the new ideology of self-sufficiency. The EC devised strategies to leapfrog ahead in terms of the most advanced products and technologies available. The first step it took towards this goal was to negotiate with multinationals such as IBM to supply computer technologies along with producing them in India. In turn, IBM and ICI, a British owned company, started to revamp used computers in Indian plants and sell or lease them to Indian customers. Whereas companies like IBM felt that Indian should evolve technologically in a step-by-step manner from one level of sophistication to another, the Electronics Committee believed that it should leap ahead to the latest technology. Thus, in a hasty move, the government tried to persuade IBM to share its equity with local capital in its Indian operations. The proposal was refused by IBM and the government, unable to impose its will, dropped the matter for the time being.

These early attempts by the government to regulate IT in India did not work as proposed and actually led to more technological backwardness as Indians were now using computers that were domestically refurbished rather than importing the latest ones. The cause for this failure was partly due to the inability to implement the strategies by the Electronics Committee, which was given to the Department of Defense Supplies along with monitoring by the newly formed Electronics Committee of India. It however, lacked the technical skills and authority needed to negotiate effectively with the MNCs or regulate the IT sector. So the government announced the formation of a Department of Electronics and a new Electronics Commission. While the Commission was responsible for formulating new policies, the Department was entrusted with the responsibility for day-to-day implementation of the devised policies. The Electronics Committee was given the authority to direct other government units, to regulate private and public electronic enterprises and develop a skilled staff capable of providing technical support. In 1975, it was given additional power over the licensing of computer imports. One of the first steps taken by the commission was the establishment of the Santa Cruz Electronics Export Processing Zone near Bombay (Mumbai). Foreign and Indian investors were encouraged to set up their export base in India along with offering various perks such as tax breaks, cheap land, duty-free import of inputs and an uncomplicated permit process. In return, the government proposed that most of the production be exported to India and maximum Indian components be utilized.

The state-run Electronics Corporation of India Ltd. (ECIL) was also set up by the government for the production of minicomputers. ECIL got almost all the funds allocated by the government for computer development, making it difficult for private companies to get operating licenses. The plan of the government was to allow imports of mainframes and large minis while allotting the small mini market to ECIL and allowing the private firms to compete in the micro sector. With these new bodies all set up, the government once again pressured IBM and ICL to dilute their equity, almost to the tune of 40%, in their Indian operations. While ICI agreed to combine its two Indian operations and reduce its equity to 40%, IBM refused again.

The government in 1975 set up the state-owned Computer Maintenance Corporation (CMC). It was entrusted with the legal monopoly of maintenance of all foreign computer systems in the country, thereby reducing the advantage presently held by IBM with its superior service capabilities. The users were now dependent on CMC irrespective of the system they purchased. This move enhanced the governments bargaining position with IBM and thus, they continued to demand that IBM dilute its 40 percent equity in Indian operations. IBM presented a proposal to instead share its equity in non-computer operations along with meet the export goals, fund an Indian science center and an electronics testing facility. Their proposal was refused by the government and after much negotiations thru and fro, IBM decided to quit India in 1978.

IBM's exit from the country clearly illustrated the government's ability in exerting its power over multinationals and thereby the development of IT industry in India. Though the aim of the government was not to drive out IBM with its stringent stand, it however, could not allow IBM to be exempted from the FERA (Foreign Exchange Regulation Act). On the other hand, IBM's departure opened up the Indian market for its various competitors such as ECIL, ICL and the Tata-Burroughs joint venture. ECIL received strong support from the government and soon dominated the market. In the late 1970s, the DOE (Department of Electronics) came under criticism for protecting ECIL at the expense of users and domestic competitors. The government then had no other choice but to give permission to several private companies such as HCL, DCM and ORG to produce data processing systems and import parts and components. This change in government policy led to the decline of ECIL, which also lagged behind in producing competitive products. And so by then, local private companies such as HCL, DCM and ORG emerged to control the market, surpassing ECIL as the major computer supplier to Indian market.

Birth of Software Industry in India

The 1970s saw the birth of the software industry in India. During the 1950s and 1960s, there was no Indian software industry. Software usually came bundled with the hardware imported by multinational hardware companies like IBM and ICL, the largest providers of hardware. Even large enterprises, including the Indian defense and public organizations that required specific software, employed an in-house team that served them customized software. The concept of stand-alone processing software did not exist. Even the local companies that emerged after IBM's exit, had their own operating systems on which only specifically designed software could be executed.

Though India was amongst the first developing counties to recognize the need for software development, it could not do so due to high import duties on hardware, which were almost 300 percent. Hence, IBM used to sell its old, refurbished machines as that was all that Indian companies could afford. Whereas, the more advanced IBM mainframe computers were standard worldwide, making it impossible for Indian software companies to design software for such advanced hardware. Within a few years, the import duties on all IT equipment were drastically brought down and then began the rise of the Indian software industry.

The first software exporting company was the Tata Consulting Services (TCS). In the late 1960s, a large conglomerate of companies known as Tata created TCS as a central service centre for Tata group companies. Around that time, with IBM out of the country, the concept of outsourcing application development work had become a necessity for Indian companies. For this, a few young professionals trained from MIT were recruited and a large computer capacity was set up. TCS began with outsourcing application work for organizations such as Central Bank of India and Bombay Telephones. Later, Tata entered into a partnership with the US organization Burroughs and a new company Tata-Burroughs was formed. TCS then began sending young Indian engineers for training to Burroughs in the US. The trainee engineers excelled at platform conversions and soon TCS started getting conversions assignments. However, after a few years of successful relationship between the two partners, there was a split due to the acquisition of Burroughs by Unisys. Thereafter the company was renamed to Tata Information System Limited and in 1969, a US trained Indian electrical engineer took over the management of TCS. He greatly promoted TCS and founded the Computer Society of India with fellow scientists and professionals and the Tata Institute of Fundamental Research. The success of TCS was followed by setting up of many new companies in India.

On one hand, a growing shortage of engineers for the fast expanding computer industry in the United States and

Europe, and on the other hand, an oversupply of Indian engineers relative to domestic demand, provided a favorable opportunity for Indian firms such as TCS and Infosys technologies to send engineers overseas for software programming onsite. Also known as "body shopping", established Indian companies supplied skilled Indian engineers to large multinationals in the IT and non-IT sectors. Body shopping was facilitated in a very organized manner with the Indian Diaspora playing a pivotal role and the liberal immigration policies in the United States at that time contributing to making it easily possible. Multinationals, primarily in the US, recruited the required programmers through local US companies such as Mastech (now iGate) and Information Management Resource. Many of these companies were established by Indians living in the US. These companies recruited these programmers through local agents. These agents would contact local agents in India, who was responsible for collecting resumes, forwarding then to the US agents, preparing visa and finalizing contracts. The programmers onsite were paid just the minimum wages allowed. On completion of their assignment, they would often move laterally to another assignment in the US through a local agent or return to India and be on the lookout for local agents to send them back again. The primary competitive advantage Indian companies had was the cost advantage and the ability to communicate using English language. The West on the other hand, faced shortage in skilled technical labor. Moreover, within the country many companies were established in India, such as Infosys, Satyam, Mastek, Silverline. They all began on a small scale by software professionals and engineers using their small savings and loans. Many were refused financial support from private banks and it was the Public Sector financial institutes who came forward and helped them with the seed money.

But in-spite of these advantages India had, its software industry faced certain challenges during the 1970s and 80s. There was a constant lack of availability of hardware as its import, especially of mainframe computers, was very expensive. There was a shortfall of trained manpower in the country. Although the education system was producing substantial number of talented engineers, very few colleges were offering any computer or IT training courses at that time. Realizing an urgent need to train Indians in IT and computers, three Indian entrepreneurs started NIIT to impart tutorials and training classes. Their early days consisted of one person driving a motorcycle and the other riding behind with a PC in his lap. They rented places in colleges and schools and offered evening classes in IT and computer courses.

Public investment in technical education began in the 1960s with the creation of elite institutes for higher education in engineering and management. Five Indian Institutes of Technology (IIT) and two Indian Institute of Management (IIM) were set up by the government in the 1960s through technical collaboration with the most industrialized countries of that time. Both these institutes attracted a large number of US trained Indian faculty. This was followed by regional engineering colleges (now known as National Institute of Technology – NIT) set up by many state governments. They attracted students from many parts of the country. All these institutes, the IIT, REC (NIT) and IIM attracted large number of applicants, and with the excellent training imparted, high calibre engineers rolled out and formed the backbone of the software industry in its early years. Many initiatives were taken by the human resource ministry to multiply technical institutes and increase technically qualified graduates. It encouraged creation of private engineering colleges and industry IT training institutions. Along with the sudden proliferation of private colleges and training institutes, the HRD ministry also devised mechanism for quality checks and control, including the establishment of an All India Council for Technical Education to regulate technical education. The Computer Society of India was also set up to monitor private training institutions. Moreover, with the introduction of a master of computer application (MCA) degree in various universities, many graduates emerged with technical and management skills required for the expanding IT industry. All these developments in the education front helped bridge the gap between the demand and supply of engineers. During the 1970s, many graduates from premier institutes such as IIT, moved to the US and other developed countries which offered then a large salary in the IT industry.

In 1993, the US immigration and Naturalization Service underwent changes, making it difficult to get B-1 visas. The new H-1 visa required a certification from the US Department of Labor that prevailing market wages were being paid to the immigrants. Because of this changes, the US companies were less in favor of attracting more immigrants and Indian software companies were additionally burdened with paying the social security and related taxes of the engineers they sent onsite. These two were major factors in bringing about a gradual move in the business model from body shopping, which involved a physical transfer of the professional to the clients office in the US or elsewhere, to a new mixed model for conducting IT business, wherein only some software programmers would work at the Clients premises (US or other nations), and the others would continue to work in the IT company's back office in India. The shift to this new model was rather gradual as the savings enjoyed by Indian companies were quite large even after sending Indian IT professions to the US. Meanwhile, IT companies continued to send software professionals to the US, UK and other countries.

Around that time came the Y2K problem and the internet-telecom boom. Y2K or the Year 2000 problem was a problem for both digital (computer-related) and non-digital documentation and data storage situations, which resulted from the practice of abbreviating a four-digit year to two digits. This Y2K problem presented a unique opportunity to Indian companies. To solve this problem, companies in the US, UK and Canada needed to hire a lot of computer programmers, causing a shortage of them in the US. Moreover, the US companies needed software professional equipped with COBOL programming skills, which had become obsolete in US university curriculum. However, in India, COBOL was still being taught. So the US government increased its H-1 visa quota and a wave of Indian IT professionals were brought to the US. The Indians in the US created a large Indian IT Diaspora in the US. Indian firms entered new markets and built trust relations with their clients. By the end of 1999, the Indian IT industry was on an all-time high and Initial Public Offerings of many Indian companies were getting oversubscribed.

Outsourcing

Body shopping referred to the physical transfer of either the programmer himself or of software in floppies. This was characteristic of the initial export years of software. In terms of products, there have been exports of enterprise systems, design software and database management tools, which formed less than 5 percent of total exports. Primarily the export was dominated by services.

In 1985, Texas Instruments (TI) set up an office in Bangalore with a direct satellite link to the US, thereby laying the foundation of the new business model of outsourcing. In 1989, an Indian Government Telecom Company (VSNL) commissioned a direct 64-kbps satellite link to the US offering software exporters a new way of operating and solving the initial problem of unreliable telecommunication links in the 1980s, which had forced Indian firms to be primarily "body shoppers". This development was paralleled by another trend of moving up the value chain from just supplying programming services to addition of design and analysis services and even offering complete turnkey projects.

Outsourcing consists of two activities – 1. Foreign companies establishing liaison, project, or branch offices in India that retain the name of the founding company; and 2. Foreign companies contracting a part of their production processes to Indian companies already formed by entering in to a "joint venture or wholly owned subsidiary". The first types of offices have a limited scope in Indian law, which prohibits branch offices of foreign companies from carrying out manufacturing activities on its own, but rather encourages then to subcontract manufacturing tasks to established Indian manufacturers.

Outsourcing of these kind became possible due to progress in technology. Advent of high-speed data connections and software tools have allowed for greater distances to be bridged and made it possible to collaborate between geographically disparate groups. This technology has also changed the structure of the production process, which was few large vertically integrated corporations in which hardware and software were produced together, to a more fragmented industrial structure allowing for production processes to be performed in various locations. These advancements in communication technology along with adequate infrastructure development, a maturing software industry and its international reputation in the last 15 years resulted in India's shift towards outsourcing. With increasing client confidence in Indian capabilities and quality standards, Indian firms moved full throttle towards offshoring. Many new companies emerged in the 1980s by entrepreneurs aiming at creating world-class software development centers.

Existing firms which had started off as subcontractors for technical manpower, gradually moved to managing complete parts or phases of projects and then further to delivering complete projects. Companies made significant efforts to deliver good practices in project management and quality and to acquire internationally recognized quality standards certification.

DESTINATION OF INDIAN SOFTWRE EXPORTS

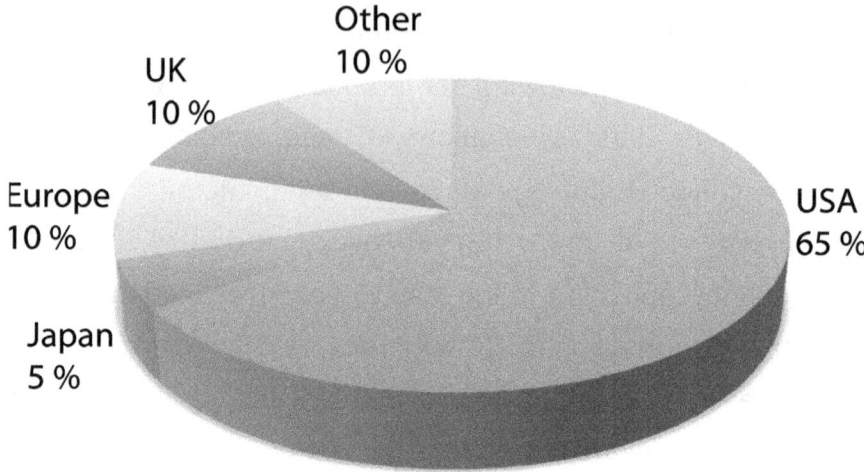

During this period, the Indian government also lent an equally supportive hand in advancing the industry and enabling offshore work in India. Various policy reforms were enacted to facilitate development of telecommunications and other infrastructure required for offshore work. It took key policy measures in the 1982 to generate optimum growth of the software industry. Various policy reforms were enacted since the late 1990s. A policy augmentation in the 1998 that ended the monopoly on Internet service provider (ISP) gateways allowed India's private sector to offer the needed bandwidth to the growing industry. Then two years later, India liberalized international long distance calling. In terms of infrastructure development, the government set up software technology parks (STPs) in 39 locations across India.

Indian Diaspora

A significant factor in the rapid development of the software sector was the success of Indian IT professions in the United States. A plethora of US educated Indian professions who had joined the IT industry in Silicon Valley had tremendous managerial and entrepreneurial success. They thus created a very positive image of the capabilities of Indian professionals. By the year 2000, almost 972 Silicon Valley technical companies were headed by Indians. By showcasing the value of Indian programmers and fostering good connections between software firms in the US and India, this Indian Diaspora also helped expedite body shopping by companies in India. While some of them returned to India to work for multinationals established as Indian subsidiaries, others set up new companies in India.

Role of Indian Government

Along with the private sector boosting the software industry in India, the government also played a very important role from constantly augmenting policies to suit the emerging software environment to generating a large and well-trained pool of engineers and management personnel who raised the Indian IT industry into a world-class industry in such a short span.

The Department of Electronics introduced a policy as early as 1972 to allow duty-free imports of computers, helping many companies in their inception stage. In the 1980, software developers were given a further boost when the Department initiated software export friendly policies. It also formed a software export promotion council and liberalized import rules for materials needed for the industry. The government policies targeted the export of software as the key sector for promotion.

In the late 1990s, the government created taskforces comprising of CEOs of leading software companies to study the software sector and recommend actions for development. At that time, the Department of Electronics became the Ministry of Communication and Information technology. Many states also began promoting the software industry by improving infrastructure, IT education and facilitating other provisions. Efforts were made by the government to attract foreign and domestic investment. Foreign companies were allowed to establish fully owned subsidiaries in the electronics export process zone. The Ministry of Finance gave greater recognition to India's comparative advantage in the sector. It removed entry barriers for foreign companies, made fast and low-cost data connection facilities available and reduced and rationalized duties, taxes and tariffs.

The Reserve Bank of India adopted several measures to support the IT industry in India, including simplification of the filing of Software Export Declaration Form (SOFTEX), acquisition of overseas parent company shares by employees of the Indian company, allowance of granting stock options to non-resident and permanent employees by companies whose software sales were over 80 percent and free remittance of foreign currency for buying services. Moreover, Indian direct investment in joint venture (JV) and wholly owned subsidiaries abroad was simplified and large investments were processed on a fast track.

Several reforms were undertaken in the telecom sector, which greatly helped accelerate the software industry. In 1998, a national telecom policy was announced to clarify the role of the regulator. It also brought about a transition from license fee to a revenue sharing model and offered domestic long distance to private operators. The ISP gateway monopoly ended in 2000, which permitted private companies to set up international gateways. Two years later, international long distance was liberalized and thus competition increased in the cellular markets brining the cost dramatically down. India's tele-density increased and cellular communication outreached landline penetration.

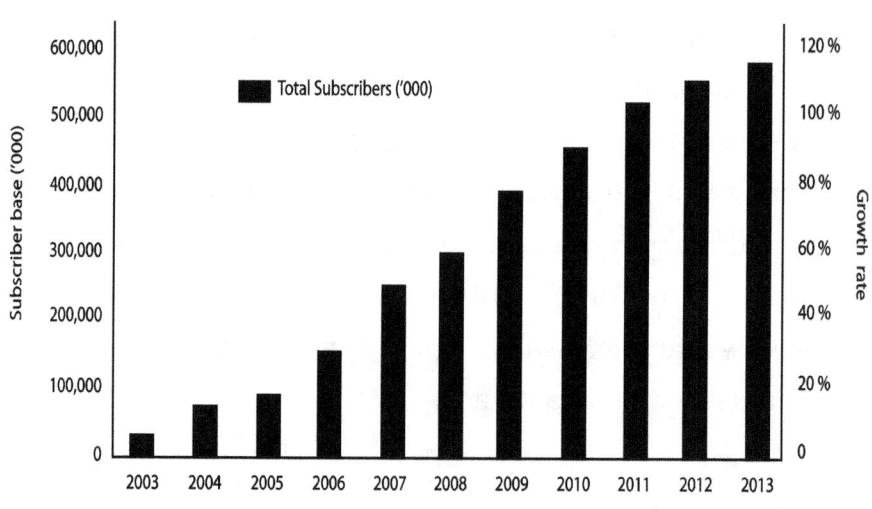

INDIA MOBILE MARKET: SUBSCRIBERS AND GROWTH RATES
(2003-2013)

Source: Frost & Sullivan
Note: All figures are rounded; the base year is 2007. MObile subscrier CAGR (2007-1013): 18.3 %

The Ministry of Human Resources Development recognized the growing need for manpower to supplement the rapidly advancing software industry and thus took many actions towards its expansion and improvement. Computer science department was created or expanded in many engineering colleges and policies enabling private sectors to open educational institutions without public funding were eased, which resulted in a large number of engineering colleges in the private sector. Quality control systems for engineering colleges and other IT training institutions were designed, such as the setting up of the All India Council for Technical Education. Along with this, accreditation system such as the Computer Society of India was set up to monitor private training institutions.

Software technology parks were established in the 1990s in 39 locations including major towns to provide infrastructure for private companies to export software. STPs provided ready-to-plug in IT and telecom infrastructure and also allowed for single-window clearance for all regulatory matters. With suitable environment, STPs enabled small and medium enterprises to come up and grow.

NUMBER OF SEZ BY STATE

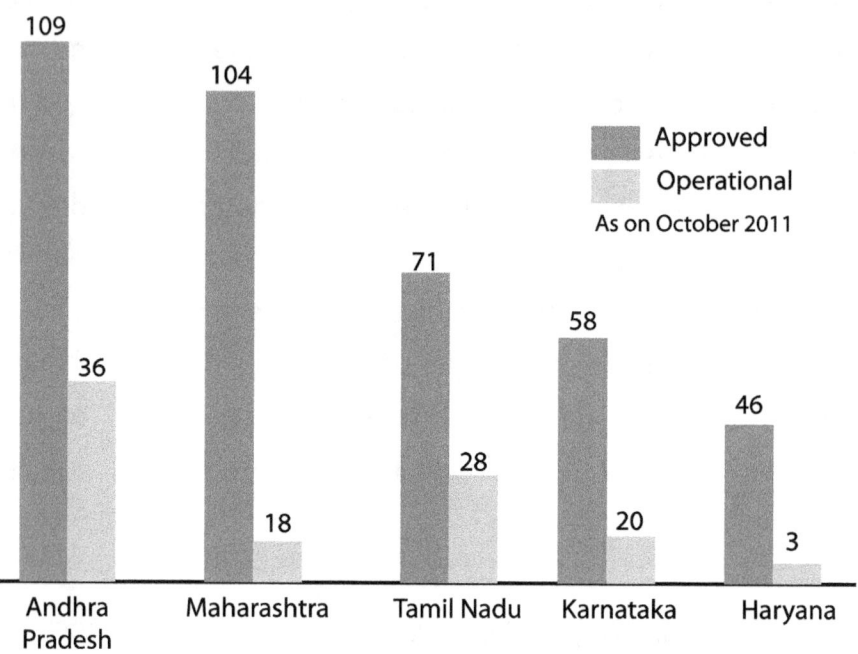

In 1988 the National Association for Service and Software Companies (NASSCOM) was founded as India's software industry association. It has been a very vocal and potent force in lobbying for many policy reforms such as rules pertaining to limiting access to capital market, issuance of stock options, easing rules on foreign currency transactions and improving the telecommunication facilities. By consistently participating in global fairs and events and organizing learning events in India featuring prominent experts from major markets,

NASSCOM has helped establish a respectable brand image of India in the global software services markets.

GDP GROWTH by sector (in %)

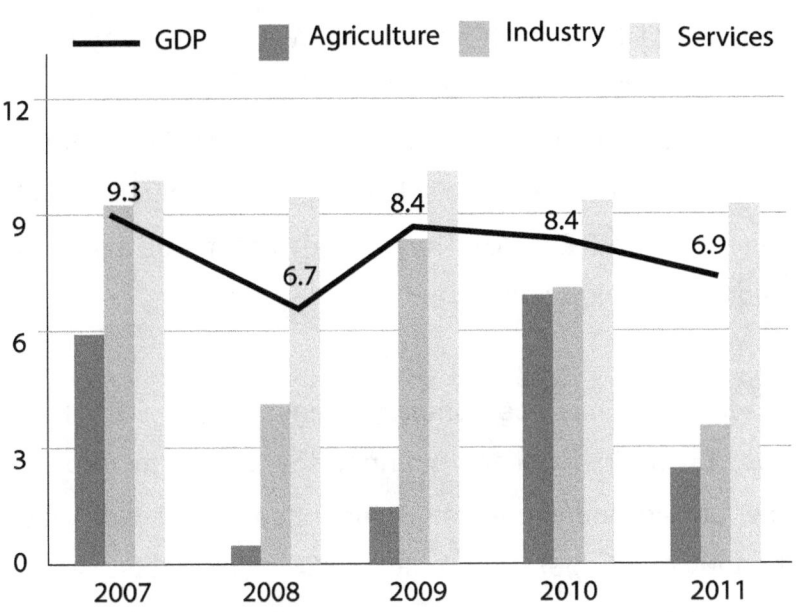

Source: Asian Development Outlook 2012

Moving up the Value Chain

Over the years, as per the International Data Corporation study, India has emerged as the fastest growing and the fourth largest IT market in Asia Pacific. It has held firm its position as the developing world's software leader. Though not very old, this industry has grown leaps in depth and scope. There are several Multinational companies which have established software development centers in India and leading Indian IT firms such as Infosys, Wipro and many other Indian multinationals have set up offices around the world, employing nationals in these countries. Some like Infosys have alliances with the world's leading firms including IBM, Intel, Microsoft and Oracle. They have even made strategic acquisitions of foreign firms.

Many traditional IT service companies have added ITES-BPO portfolios to their existing offerings in order to provide complete end-to-end services. Some have increased Multi-vendor and build-operate-transfer (BOT) contracts, which offer customers advantages such as low risk, scalability and competitive pricing. Indian vendors are expanding the spectrum of their service offerings in client locations and even setting up facilities in other low cost ITES-BPO destinations such as China and the Philippines in order to tap the potential of these new markets.

Leading firms have moved up the value chain in software services by developing effective organizational and managerial capabilities that enable then to offer more comprehensive services than just low cost programming. Today's industries increasingly procure fixed price contracts rather than the time-and-material contracts of earlier years, signaling a maturity of the Indian software industry. This has brought about flexibility in organizing work, greater management control and an opportunity to earn higher returns as efficiency improves. A move up the value chain has also brought about increased revenue per worker. To establish good client value, companies have gone an extra step to expand their capacity to service a wider range of software development tasks as well as moved in to new services such as product design and Information Services outsourcing. Indian companies are moving beyond writing and testing, which requires least skills and accounts for only a small portion of the overall project cost, to works which require higher skill levels and deeper business knowledge. But along with the quest to move up the value chain, Indian software companies have ensured quality and reliability of product. They have adopted internationally recognized standardized work processes and many companies have met international certification requirements. Most of the software companies in India are very young, but they introduced quality checks and system very soon after being formed.

Indian vendors have moved beyond call centers and into financial services, telecom, retailing and automotive segments of the ITES-BPO sector. For example, in the financial sector, Indian companies are offering customers services centered around accounting, billing and payment services and transaction processing. Some Indian service providers have also been offering higher value services to customers in the areas of insurance claims processing and equity research support. These companies expect to gain from the offshoring-outsourcing of customer and technical support, product development by global telecom industry, process of transaction processing, billing, telemarketing and inventory management of large retailers, engineering activities such as computer aided product and tool designs, claims processing and accounting processes of automobile industry.

Today Indian software companies attract the best of talent from engineering schools. Indian employees are ambitious and look for constant improvements in the way the organization work.

Recognizing the huge potential of Indian software companies, leading global companies (Indian as well as MNC) are also focusing some of their attention towards tapping the domestic market. Revenue earned from the domestic market by export centered Indian service providers has grown and several of the key IT outsourcing contracts awarded in the past years have been won by MNCs.

TRANSITION IN SERVICE MIX

Top service offerings in 2011	Promising service offerings in 2012-13
1. Customer Care & Contact Centre Services	1. Research & Analytics
2. Data Capture/Management	2. Customer Interaction & Support Services
3. Document Management	3. Insurance Claim Processing
4. Email Support	4. Finance & Accounting
5. Insurance Claim Processing	5. Engineering & R&D
6. Card/Cheque Processing	6. HR Processing Services
7. Human Resource Services	7. Testing Services
8. Payroll Processing	8. CADM
9. Tele-marketing	9. Procurement Services
10. Market Research & Analysis	10. Document Management

Source: D&B Research

Global product companies are even working out to introduce localized versions of their software products to drive up usability. This specific focus on the domestic business opportunity is helping create a healthy competitive environment.

ESTIMATED SIZE OF INDIAN IT AND ITES INDUSTRY BY 2022

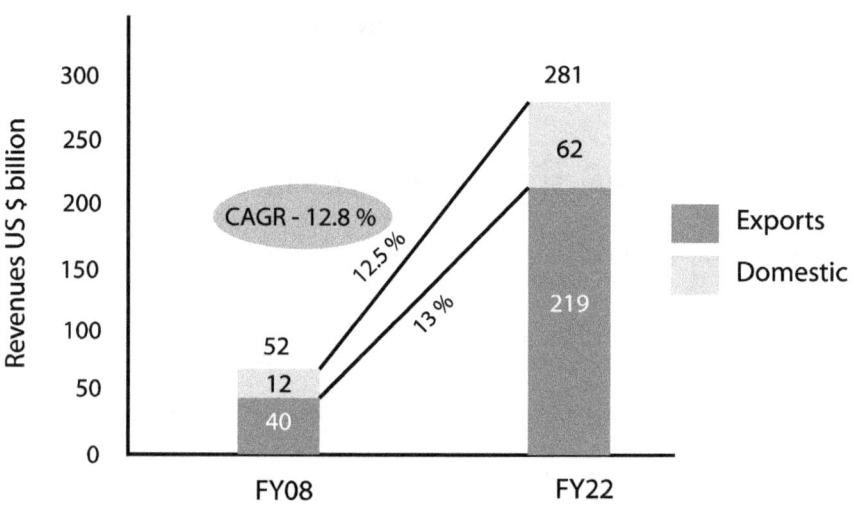

Source: NASSCOM 2020 Prespective and IMaCS analysis

The Indian IT software industry has had wide-ranging effects across the economy. Various policy changes to cater to the fast changing environment of the software industry in turn facilitated the rapid development of a domestic IT market. It also brought about increasing efficiency due to adoption of information technologies. Indian businesses, government and consumers have ready access to the newest software products and imported hardware. Indian IT firms have set high standards of management and adopted practices of creative organizations with less hierarchical structures and strong work ethics, thereby pioneering a movement to modernize Indian management practices.

In order to comply with international norms and participate in international capital markets, IT firms have set new standards in accounting and corporate government. Tremendous employment opportunities offered by the software industry, which are high-paying for the young and educated, has had a significant effect on the confidence, aspirations and work ethics of young professionals.

There are various factors that explain the success of India's software industry. While India had an early mover advantage in this industry, its repeated positive experience and building of long lasting trust relations with its clients has played a crucial role in validating India as a brand today. No dearth of human capital resource including software engineers, project managers and corporate leaders has been ideal for setting up the software industry, which is entirely built on human capital and requires limited infrastructure and upfront investment. Timely investments by the government towards education of

IT and simultaneous encouragement to private sector for the same, has ensured a constant supply of skilled manpower resource. Augmentation of policies at every required stage of the industry by government, bureaucrats and NASSCOM, which meant removal of constraints and barriers, has acted as a supporting hand to the Indian software companies.

Thus as compared to its competitors in this industry, India ranks high on these critical parameters such as level of government support, strong track record of quality and timely delivery, talented labor pool with English speaking advantage, effective project management skills and a favorable time zone difference with the US that allows for 24/7 operations. However, there are some weaknesses that persist in the Indian Software industry. The domestic market is slow growing and the large number of small and medium sized companies severely lack innovation and product orientation. Moreover, infrastructure needs improvement in areas such as roads, electricity, venture capital and airports. Market concentration continues to be North America and is therefore subject to non-tariff barriers such as visa denials.

		THE A.T KEARNEY GLOBAL SERVICES LOCATION INDEX,™ 2011			
Rank	Country	Financial Attractive-ness	People Skills & Availabil-ity	Business environ-ment	Total score:
1	India	3.11	2.76	1.14	7.01
2	China	2.62	2.55	1.31	6.49
3	Malaysia	2.78	1.38	1.83	5.99
4	Egypt	3.10	1.36	1.35	5.81
5	Indonesia	3.24	1.53	1.01	5.78
6	Mexico	2.68	1.60	1.44	5.72
7	Thailand	3.05	1.38	1.29	5.72
8	Vietnam	3.27	1.19	1.24	5.69
9	Philippines	3.18	1.31	1.16	5.65
10	Chile	2.44	1.27	1.82	5.52
11	Estonia	2.31	0.95	2.24	5.51
12	Brazil	2.02	2.07	1.38	5.48
13	Latvia	2.56	0.93	1.96	5.46
14	Lithuania	2.48	0.93	2.02	5.43
15	UAE	2.41	0.94	2.05	5.41
16	UK	0.91	2.26	2.23	5.41
17	Bulgaria	2.82	0.88	1.67	5.37
18	USA	0.45	2.88	2.01	5.35
19	Costa Rica	2.84	0.94	1.56	5.34

Source: The A.T Kearney Global Services Location Index,™ 2011

CHANGE NEEDED IN INDIAN IT

Recent industry trends are clear indicators of the fact that Indian IT companies have dwelled rather too long on past successes instead of looking forward and preparing for the future. Growth and Profit margins of over 25% has become the industry norm. Instead of planning, developing credible intellectual properties through meaningful research and development and investing in the future, the pressure to maintain profits and growth has pushed all these
companies on their tried and tested traditional path of body shopping. Now, when countries like China and US have moved ahead with innovations, helping businesses globally to generate better cost savings than the traditional models, the worst hit will be the Indian IT sector. This issue is compounded by the global economic slowdown, which is hitting every country equally hard.

The success of Indian firms and professionals in the

information technology (IT) arena during the last decade has

been spectacular. India has been riding high on the IT

bandwagon and has leapfrogged into a knowledge-based

economy. Instances of people in remote villages sending and receiving email
messages or surfing the Internet are mere examples of how India has transformed technologically. Increasing population with access to computers and the Internet and e-governance is being projected as the way of the future. The Indian information technology industry is poised to become a US$ 225 billion industry by 2020 and secure a prominent position on the global map. This rapid expansion of the Indian IT industry has been a key feature of economic development in India and worldwide. The Indian IT industry has become a main source for export earnings and also a key driver in the transformation of the domestic economy. India has emerged as a major centre for offshoring of IT services.

The Indian IT Sector generated more than $100 billion in revenues in 2011-12 and NASSCOM has projected an aggressive growth of more than 13% for 2012-13.

Software companies have been projecting impressive growth over the past two decades. The IT-BPO sector too has become one of the most significant growth catalysts for the Indian economy. It is fueling India's economy to a great extent and is also positively influencing the lives of many people through an active direct and indirect contribution to various socio-economic parameters such as employment generation, improving standard of living and creation of diverse opportunities. The industry has played a significant role in transforming India's image from a slow moving bureaucratic economy to a land of innovative entrepreneurs. India can now boast of being a global player in providing world-class technology solutions and business services.

The Information technology industry in India has gained a brand identity as a knowledge economy due to its IT and ITES sector. It has led to the growth in the service sector in India and has contributed substantially to increase in GDP, employment, and exports. Export dominates the IT–ITES industry, and constitutes about 77% of the total industry revenue. According to NASSCOM, the IT–BPO sector in India aggregated revenues of US$88.1 billion in FY2011. Bangalore, Chennai, Hyderabad, Mumbai, Pune, Delhi, Kolkata and Coimbatore account for about 90% of this sector's exports.

Besides exports, this sector has also brought about employment generation through direct employment in the IT services and BPO/ITES segment, which was pegged at 2.3

million in the year 2009-10 and is estimated to reach nearly 2.5 million by the end of financial year 2010-11; and through Indirect employment of over 8.3 million job opportunities.

GDP growth outlook: India on firm ground

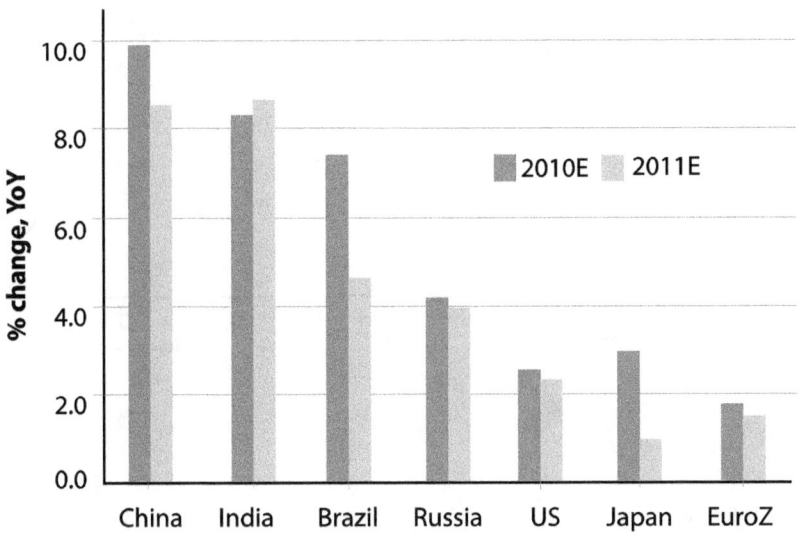

Source: The Economist

However, this unstoppable growth until now is showing signs of slowdown. The honeymoon period for the Indian IT industry is drawing to a close. Though enjoying the benefits of growth in the IT and BPO segment, the Indian IT industry is witnessing what could be termed as 'problems of growth'.

INDIAN RUPEES (INR) TO 1 US DOLLAR (USD)

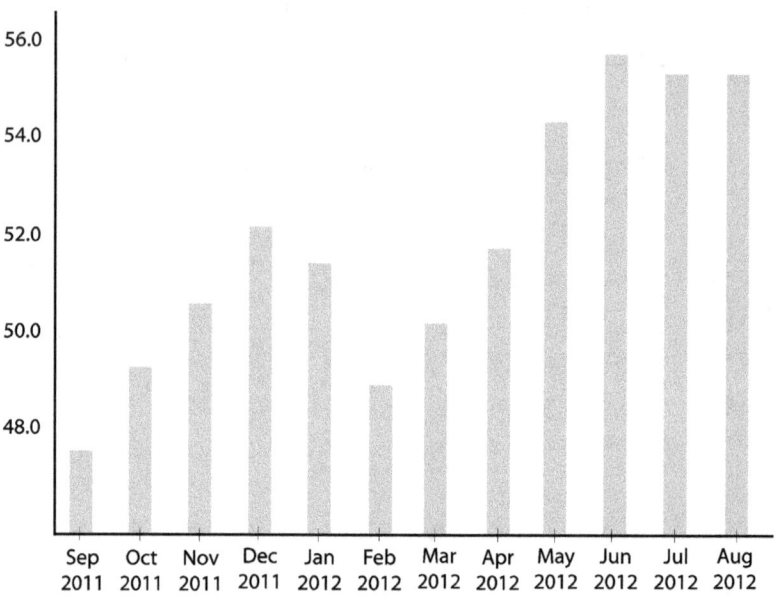

Source: www.exchange-rates.org

While India can still boast of assets like a talented pool of people who are technically competent and linguistically better at English compared to the other competitors/countries, government support, large work force, sufficient infrastructure, effective educational system, cost benefit, cultural compatibility, global and legal maturity, and data and intellectual property security and privacy, these assets are now becoming roadblocks to further growth, development and success as the business environment evolves and moves up the value chain. According to a NASSCOM survey, majority of college graduates today are unemployable, lacking passion, competence and soft skills.

In the wake of the economic recession in the US, which started in 2007 and continues in some form or the other, IT expenditures have been drastically cut and the companies in India are facing a lot of heat as majority of these companies have an export driven business model with maximum exports to the US.

Besides, new competitive markets have emerged in Latin America, Eastern Europe and South East Asia to take advantages of cost-effectiveness along with benefits of proximity to their major business clientele in the USA.

The rupee fluctuations due to a weakened US economy and Indian economy problems has caused IT companies in India to book lower profit margins at times and higher at other times. While the government has extended a helping hand throughout and contributed greatly to the development of IT in India, it needs to put in some more effort to balance the fluctuations and the consequent effects of it and keep the wheels of IT development constantly churning.

Anti-offshoring sentiments and protectionism from USA and Europe are threatening Indian companies with potential loss of clients and profits. India too has been witnessing rising cost due to high inflation and interest rates. Onsite positions, which once promised good cash flows for Indian IT companies are now an expensive proposition and a burden on companies.

The government needs to take steps to manage excess FDI inflows into the country and hedge the export driven sectors against rupee fluctuations. It needs to develop more IT SEZs to reduce the excess tax burden on IT companies. DTA (domestic Tariff Areas) norms need sufficient relaxation to promote IT spending in the country.

Moreover, majority of the IT clientele is in the BFSI (Banking Financial Sector and Insurance) sector, which has borne the maximum brunt of recession. With the BFSI clients cutting down their IT spending, Indian companies need to make their presence in various other verticals to make themselves immune to such eventualities.

While the software industry is the focus of Indian IT, the hardware industry is lagging way behind leaving a huge gap on solution providing, which is now getting more and more hardware centric. Besides challenges of complicated local indirect tax structure and high rates of excise and sales taxes, the hardware sector is not encouraged to undertake R&D by offering incentives such as 150 percent write off on R&D expenditures, which is offered to other sectors such as pharmaceuticals and manufacturing. While India performs numerous hardware assembly tasks internally, it is entirely for the domestic market and import of hardware is usually from the South East or East Asian counties. There is also a need to improve labor laws to boost the hardware sector which would lead to increased employment and productivity. Against the background of iPhones and Tablets becoming mainstream in technology, India has no role to play in the same. India is taking a backstage in new technologies due to the absence of any hardware focus.

Thus, increased competition from emerging IT locations, falling profit margins, shaky global economy and dearth of talent are some of the reasons which have emerged as the foremost challenges in the current Indian IT scene. Besides other challenges such as data security issues, currency fluctuations, cultural issues and general business ethics, are also affecting the Indian IT industry.

IT industry in India is much pampered by the government in terms of benefits, directly and indirectly, because of which, it has had a free run since the last two decades, barring a brief period during the dot com bust and the 2007 recession. But the industry, behest with many challenges and problems of growth, is now staring at a not so bright future. Almost all companies have experienced more than average business losses with customers moving out due to reasons of budget cuts, getting a better deal or even opting out for their own captive company in India. Most of the mid and small scale companies are now struggling to keep employee ranks intact and have been plagued with an average 25% attrition rate. Moreover, from 2010 to 2012, many companies, such as Infosys and Wipro, have laid-off many employees who were on bench and have also stalled salary hikes. The advantages the industry once enjoyed in its initial stages of development through government and other benefits, have now become roadblocks and problems of growth. While these factors contributed to rapid advancement, with time, these very factors are becoming problems and challenges.

Problems facing the country are grimmer than envisaged. While the huge machinery of colleges continue to churn out more than 100000 engineering graduates annually, many students may not find jobs and those with jobs may find it hard looking for work within their organization due to reduction in business opportunities, thus creating a grave situation of joblessness. Huge requirements for commodity skills in the market over the last few years has resulted in substandard skills being accepted. Re-training such employees to improve productivity will not be easy and cannot be done quickly. In all, lack of foresight and preparedness for such challenges is a big risk, which the Indian IT companies have left unmitigated.

Issues of Government Policies in India

The story of the Indian software industry began as a private initiative with government support towards IT prevalent from the early beginnings of the industry in terms of public funding, provision for training and education of engineers and management personnel, simplifying and easing out the labyrinth of regulations and devising policies in favor of the growth and development of IT in the country. In fact, it can be said that the biggest beneficiary of government policies have been the IT and ITeS sectors leading to its unprecedented growth in the past decade.

During the 70's, the country did not witness major developments in the IT industry due to restrictive imports of computer peripherals, high import tax and the strict Foreign Exchange and Regulation Act. Post 1984, policy reforms were devised to recognize software as an industry to develop and thus brought about various incentives such as reduced import tariffs and increased exposure to the latest technologies so that Indian companies could compete globally and capture a share of global software exports. During this period, all state-owned banks were standardizing banking processes and there came a need for using UNIX over MS-DOS, thereby making India a "Unix country". The Department of Electronics (DoE) set up in the 1990s introduced the concept of Software Technology Park (STPs), which were allocated basic infrastructure, dependable power supply, tax exemptions and also given 100% ownership for foreign firms. The Government introduced policies which liberalized FDI, provided sufficient tax exemptions, basic infrastructure like STP's, subsidies in energy resources, single window system and support by local state governments for attracting MNC's. Along with the incentives, support industries, such as security services, HR payroll, recruitment and logistics were also given a boost, creating a favorable environment for IT growth. Venture capitalists and private equity providers encouraged local entrepreneurs to develop their ideas to create global companies. Enactment of the Information Technology Act, 2000 by the Indian government now acts as a framework to address legal issues and security concerns related to computer crimes and IT protection. Both the central and state government are providing investments for infrastructures, training centers and testing laboratories. There has also been a drastic cut on bureaucratic interference. India also has NASSCOM, which provides a blue print of the needs and progress path of IT vendors and IT companies in India.

Thus, the Indian IT industry is replete with examples of aid provided by the government in many areas, which has led to a tremendous growth of the industry. But while these companies have been able to reap benefits from these initiatives, there are areas where government support and incentives are lacking or inadequate, but are equally required to allow for the continuous and problem-free growth of the industry. The Indian IT industry still lacks many of the other benefits provided to other industries such as manufacturing and pharmaceuticals. While the software industry is well taken care of, the hardware segment of the IT industry has not received enough support by the government. It has therefore, not shown the same level of progress as ITES and software. The hardware industry has to deal with complications in local indirect tax structure and high rates of excise and sales taxes. Moreover, while industries such as pharmaceuticals and automobile companies are encouraged to carry out research and development activities through a 150 percent write-off on expenditure, no such facility is extended to the IT hardware industry. Also, labor laws have been amended for IT services and software, but no such initiative has been taken for the hardware segment. Manufacturing semiconductors and other sophisticated hardware components profitably, requires infrastructure and large scale investments in building capacity, and this is where India is lagging behind. Hardware components are usually imported from the Southeast or East Asian countries. The design of hardware typically involves the development and use of appropriate software codes and thus, hardware design can be a promising area for the Indian IT sector. There is also a need to bring about flexible labor laws, because the employment elasticity of output growth is declining. Flexible and transparent laws are the need of the hour for increased employment and productivity and to realize the full benefits of growth in the IT sector.

India attracts bulk of the global ITES-BPO sector mainly due to its comparative advantage in terms of price, performance and quality. But despite the high export growth, the domestic market only represents a small percentage of the industry, which is negligible in comparison to the exports. High piracy levels, pressure on software processes and low IT spending by domestic companies are some of the factors responsible for the lag in the domestic IT service and software segment.

INDIAN IT BPO REVENUE

IT-BPO Segment	FY2008 (US$ mn)			FY2009 (US$ mn)			FY2010 (US$ mn)		
	Exports	Domestic	Total	Exports	Domestic	Total	Exports	Domestic	Total
IT Services	22,203	7,882	30,085	25,800	8,226	34,026	27,290	8,940	36,230
BPO	9,915	1,576	11,491	11,703	1,932	13,635	12,401	2,288	14,689
Software Products & Engineering Services	8,300	2,234	10,534	9,600	2,690	12,290	9,999	2,771	12,770
Hardware	500	10,293	10,793	395	9,006	9,401	395	9,002	9,397
Total	40,918	21,985	62,903	47,498	21,854	69,352	50,085	23,001	73,086

Source: NASSCOM

The R&D incentives provided by the government to the IT industry constitutes a miserly fraction of the revenues earned and is insufficient when compared to other industries such as automobile, manufacturing and pharmaceuticals. R&D is needed by the IT industry to pinpoint future trends, predict business and technology requirements, and develop a strong sales and marketing network. India has been recognized as having a huge R&D potential by many MNCs, with more than 300 setting up their R&D and technical centers. According to several international surveys, India is the preferred destination for setting up innovation centers. One of the main advantages India offers is the low cost of talent. The total annual payroll cost of an Indian scientist or engineer is about $22,600 per annum as compared to $90,000 per annum in the US, which is almost a quarter of the cost in US. However, even though R&D investment has recorded an increase over the years, the government and private sector companies are yet to exploit its full potential to Indian advantage. In the R&D sphere, private participation has been minimal and most programs have been initiated by the government. The government initiatives are marred by stumbling blocks of complex, overlapping structures of policy making and decision making, rigid, bureaucratic resource allocation procedures and lack of clear accountability. Over the years, Indian IT and software companies have contributed more towards R&D spending from almost nothing in 1991 to 1.5 percent of sales by the year 2004. But even then, large software companies like Wipro and Infosys have not increased their R&D spending significantly. The public sector accounts for 70-80 percent of India's total R&D spend, which is about 0.8 percent of GDP. Relative to India's economic size and international context, this amount is very low. Growth of R&D activities in India holds a promising spillover to the Indian economy. With more and more new enterprises being set up, Indian scientist and engineers will gain greater expertise and experience. Besides, it is a good demonstration of Indian assets and capabilities in the R&D field, which can be effectively exploited.

Majority of the firms in India are based at the lower level of the value pyramid that is body shopping and offshore development. Most Indian software firms are hesitant to take high-risk high-return strategies and hence, stick to more conservative strategies. But in order to move up the value chain, Indian companies need to get more involved in R&D activities, product creation, brand management and strategic consulting, areas where there is hardly any focus being accorded even by cash rich companies. For example, Infosys started out with the body shopping and offshoring business model 30 years ago. At that time, there was an immediate requirement to focus on such activities as it filled a huge gap on the client's supply side, and generated huge profits for Indian outsourcing companies and signaled the IT revolution in India. Over the years, factors such as decreasing cost competitiveness, rising operations cost and changing global technology needs and business models has shifted body shopping and offshoring to the backseat and moved IP creation, innovation and acquisition to the forefront. However, with little effort made towards developing these future trends, Infosys and many other IT companies in India have continued on the earlier business models, especially due to the large profit benefits. Now, 30 years later, with the outsourcing pie rapidly shrinking and all companies fighting for the same share, many are facing the heat of losing business contracts and have now realized the urgent need to move up the value chain.

The various tax benefits provided to the industry has certainly helped companies expand quickly and accumulate large capital. But the tax incentives have helped in achieving just that – accumulation of large sums of capital. There has been little encouragement from the government to re-invest the capital for its continuous generation, or investment of capital for R&D activities, which can help companies move up the value chain from mere body shopping and offshoring to creation of intellectual property. Models of body shopping and offshoring are now slowly becoming redundant with increasing prices and reducing profitability. With client contracts decreasing, leading to companies fighting for the same pie, there is an urgent need to change gears towards new models of business with focus on IP creation in order to retain the growth so far witnessed by the IT industry in India.

Issues of Education

India boasts of the largest 'Higher Education System' in the world. Over the years, the Indian Technical Education Sector has grown many folds and developed a number of approaches to assure and improve its quality. India has produced many eminent and competent technocrats who have been responsible for many innovations not only in India but all over the world. India is the largest producer of scientific and professional manpower and has strongly established its competitive advantage in the knowledge-led business economy.

University Students Graduating in Science and Technology

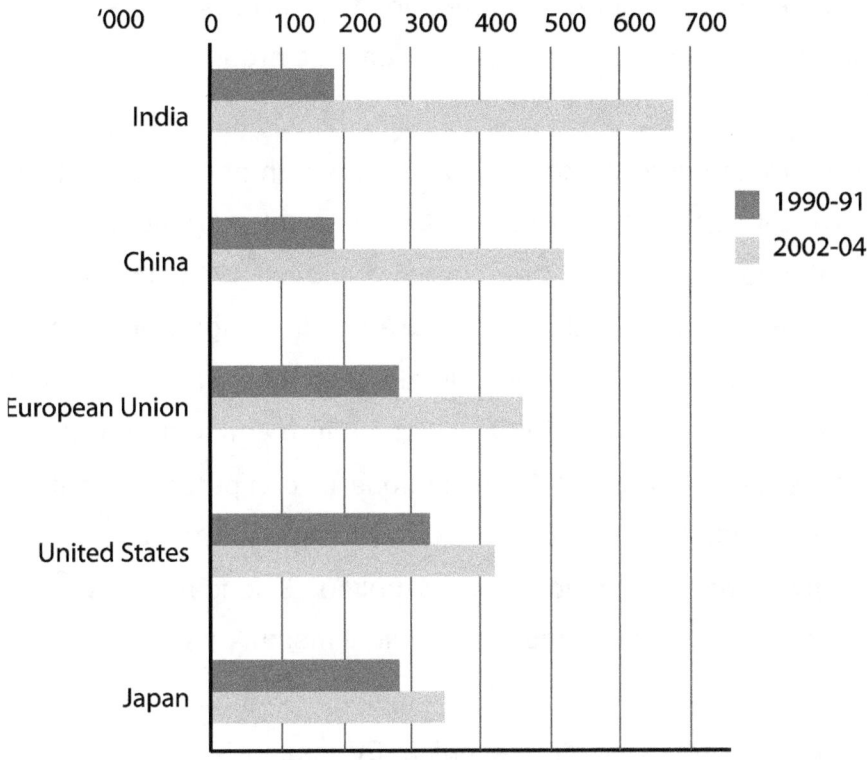

Source: Morgan Stanley

Technical education, especially engineering, has seen increasing enrollments over the last decades, making India the leading offshore destination. As a result, India stands at 65 percent of the global IT offshore industry and 46 percent of the global Business Process Off shoring (BPO) industry. Technical education is imparted at various levels such as:

craftsmanship, diploma, degree, post-graduate and research in specialized fields, catering to various aspects of technological development and economic progress.

The government sector, private and voluntary organizations have all contributed to setting up technical and management Institutes throughout the country. Today, 1764 institutions conduct Post Graduate Programs in Engineering and Technology with an annual intake capacity of 31,621; and 1147 institutions impart PG Programs in management with an intake of 0.1 million; 953 institutions in computer application with an intake of 67637. Facilities for doctoral studies in Engineering, Technology and Applied Sciences have also been created in a number of technical institutions.

The All India Council for Technical Education (AICTE) was set up in 1945 as an advisory body and in 1987 it was given the statutory status by an Act of Parliament. It serves as an advisory body for engineering and technology educational institutions including planning and coordinating development. Its vision is to become a world-class organization leading technological and socioeconomic development of the country by enhancing the global competitiveness of technical manpower and by ensuring high quality technical education to all sections of the society. However, even with all the encouragement given by the government and the effective establishment of IT education in the country, it is currently behest with numerous problems, which are now posing a challenge to the IT sector.

One of the most glaring problems today is that of a shortage of skilled technical workers. It is estimated that that engineering colleges in India have seats for 1.5 million students, nearly four times the 390,000 available in 2000, but 75% of technical graduates and more than 85% of general graduates are unemployable in India's global industries, including information technology and call centers. This leaves about 25 percent technical graduates and 10-15 percent general college graduates suitable for employment in the IT and BPO industries. IT graduates are attracted to companies for the easy money and a simple method of going abroad, and this shows in their output in terms of missed delivery dates, faulty codes and resulting frustration from clients. They lack the passion and drive for constant innovation and improvements. Sustainable success in the global market will require highly skilled and knowledgeable workforce, who are passionate and motivated about work.

Indian higher education sector is also plagued by severe shortage of teaching staff, posing a threat to the quality of the large knowledge seeking population. Low pay, lack of facilities, massive expansion of higher education institutions with a poor supply of PhDs, delay in recruitment, lack of incentives to attract and nurture talent are some of the grave issues facing the higher education sector. The rapid increase in the number of technical institutions has not been proportionate to the rise in faculty. For example, while the government has decided to increase the number of IIT from 7 to 15, along with significantly increasing the number of students to meet all the quotas, efforts to increase the faculty to serve the growth has been minimal. So where there should have been one faculty for every 10 students, the ratio is now one to 450 students, thus a compromise on the quality of teaching. Small-scale private colleges account for the bulk of IT training institutes, which are merely money-making enterprises with chunks of professors unqualified to impart expertise. Along with quantity, the quality of the faculty also needs to improve, as most do not even have the required level of experience and qualification.

With growth projections being hazy now, aggressive growth in new world will require fundamentally different skill sets than what is seen today. Keeping in view the aggressive growth projections of the IT industry, India needs an additional 300000 employees, and thus, with the present state of graduates fit for IT, there is a gap between the demand and supply of IT manpower. It is very essential to improve the quality of higher education in general and in line with the IT industry's requirements in particular to avoid non-availability of human capital becoming a bottleneck for the growth of this sector. There is a need for universities to take effective measures to bridge the gap between academia and industry.

Price distortions, lack of physical and human capital infrastructure, obsolete curriculum, government interventions, ineffective regulatory body and lack of encouragement for public-private partnership are reasons for the poor state of higher education in the country. While this calls for increasing enrollments in the colleges and opening of new colleges, it also needs upscaling of quality through course augmentation with better educational standards and well-trained faculty. Many universities, especially the state funded ones, still follow the course curriculum designed during the 1960s and 1970s. Against the fast changing skill requirements to meet the evolving technical needs, the curriculum too needs to constantly evolve to remain effective in imparting the most up-to-date education and inculcate in students the habit of learning throughout their lives. The University Grants Commission (UGC) and the All India Council for Technical Education, the two most powerful regulators and disbursers of the government grants for higher education are left with little credibility in the market to enforce an effective education structure. Higher education needs a reduction in government control and allocation of greater autonomy in order to bring about drastic changes required to modernize and scale it up to meet the demands of the rapidly expanding economy. Extensive cooperation between public and private sector would further enhance the quality of education. Industry help should be sought to bring about industry and academic partnership and to benefit from industry expert knowledge and expertise. Education should be upgraded to include research and should support innovation and conventional teaching to meet the diverse requirements of the transforming industry. Along with rapid and extensive quantitative growth, there is a need for appropriate and effective qualitative evaluation of IT education.

Moreover, there is no flexibility in IT education in terms of transnational education and distance learning/virtual universities, which can make technical education available to various parts of the country, even if there are no established training institutions in that area. This will help generate more graduates.

In India, only about 7.2 percent of adults in the age group of 17-24 have the privilege of getting higher education. This means that about 10.5 million - just 11% of the total relevant age group – enroll for higher education. On this count, India fares poorly compared to South East Asian countries like Philippines (31%), Thailand (19%), Malaysia (27%) and China (13%). The country's public expenditure on higher education is among the lowest in the world, with only $406 per student, as compared to China ($2,728), Brazil ($3,986), Indonesia ($666) and Malaysia ($625). Thus, there is an urgent need to enlarge the role and relevance of our universities and technical institutions to generate more skilled workforce. The various government tax benefits aimed at the IT Industry have given cash benefits to these organizations. But in return, these organizations have extended very little support in developing the education sector, and even the demands from these companies for more and more graduates did in no way result in world class colleges funded by them. Companies need to be encouraged to contribute towards development of such assets so that the supply of skilled workforce does not hamper their growth.

Business outlook

The Indian IT industry had a humble beginning in the 1970s and throughout the 1980s grew at a moderate pace, even though it faced many challenges related to government policies, infrastructure, education training and hardware. The industry witnessed its boom during the time of the Y2K problem, which presented Indian companies with a unique opportunity. To solve the Y2K problem, companies in the US, UK and Canada needed to hire computer programmers in vast numbers, resulting in manpower shortage in the US. Moreover, the US companies needed software professionals equipped with COBOL programming skills, which was obsolete in US university curriculum, but in India, COBOL was still being taught. Thus, this gap in the information technology at that time, was used as an opportunity by India to utilize its manpower resources. This led to the US government increasing its H-1 visa quota, which was followed by a wave of Indian IT professionals moving to the US. The Indians in the US created a large Indian IT Diaspora in the US. By the end of 1999, the Indian IT industry was at its all-time high. The US educated Indian professionals joined the IT industry in the US. Showcasing their technical, managerial and entrepreneurial skills and success, they created a positive image of Indian professionals' capabilities. By the year 2000, nearly 972 Silicon Valley technology companies were headed by Indians, accounting for 26,000 jobs. The Indian Diaspora helped expedite body-shopping by fostering connections between software firms in the US and India. Multinationals in the US recruited Indian programmers through placement firms such as Mastech (now iGate) and Information Management Resource based in the US and established and operated by Indians living there. Some Indians returned to India to work for Indian subsidiaries of multinationals, while some started their own firms in the US or India.

Whenever there were gaps in the industry, be it in terms of the shortage of skilled workforce during the Y2K phase or be it the need for body shopping and outsourcing for cost benefit, opportunities were created by Indians, either living in the US or back home, to fill those gaps, and in the process, bring about the IT industry revolution. However, since the beginning, the focus of IT in India has been to merely do that – to fill in the gaps. While the Y2K problem was short-lived, body shopping business model provided a constant supply of companies as it benefited the companies with the most important factor of cutting down the cost. And with Indian vendors getting the big bucks, they felt little need to move their focus from this business model. So companies after companies were established in India, each involved in body shopping.

In recent times, however, due to the US economy downturn, companies are now reviewing their IT spending and forcing their vendors, mostly in India, to become more flexible in business. So, instead of substantial and upfront capital spending, new payment models that allow spending in the form of operating expenditures and payment for on-demand usage are forcing Indian IT and BPO firms to find new business models and to move away from body-shop roots. Besides, anti-offshoring sentiments in the US and other European countries, which are now resorting to protectionism, are leading to loss of contracts for Indian companies. Many companies are setting up their captive units in India, resulting in loss of revenue and high competition for talent within firms.

Moreover, efforts to bring about significant innovations in self-developed products or business models have been only minuscule by Indian companies. India has not yet realized its full potential for innovation. This is partly because the education and research institutes do not encourage a culture of experimentation and exchange of ideas and partly because of the low risk taking appetite of Indians. The government too, has not encouraged R&D to inculcate the practice of innovative thinking. Education, right from the beginning, is more of a culture of "learn-what-is-told" rather than "learn-on-your-own-with-experiments". It lacks encouragement to think, innovate and experiment.

Cultural issues

The business culture of a country is to a great extent dependent on the traditional values and beliefs of that country, which are not easily swayed. In India too, the business attitude and outlook of people is vastly influenced by its culture. This in turn shapes the industrial development of the country, in a mould made of the outlook and beliefs based on culture.

For example, American culture encourages new technology as they believe it leads to progress, and that optimism leads to a better future. They believe that change is usually for the better and thus, are more accepting of changes and culturally do not fear rapid advancement. This attitude has led to undertaking high-risk ventures, involving constant innovation and utilization of new technology. Indians, deeply rooted in traditional culture and values, fear "Americanization", which they feel is brought about by globalization to countries. They in general fear high-risk initiatives and are often stuck to the 'settled mind-set' of having a job and income security and with less inclination towards entrepreneurial undertakings. America, been mired in mostly a red-hot economy, demonstrates a "growth mind-set", perfectly suitable for nurturing entrepreneurs.

When the IT wave hit India, companies were formed to supply to the gap in the processes of US companies. For this purpose, skilled workers were churned out to work for companies in the West as it was the urgent need of the hour. They moved to body shopping, again filling in for the need of the companies abroad. All this did pave the way for the IT revolution in India, greatly supplementing the economic progress, creating jobs and opportunities for millions and ushering in the era of technological advancement in India. But with time, with countries becoming more self-sufficient in terms of producing the required skilled labor, and other factors such as increasing cost of outsourcing and the overall economic gloom, India has been caught in a position where it has only body shopping and offshoring to offer, as that had been its focus all the while. While it has amassed capital, it is now finding it difficult to channelize this capital for further advancement. India values persistence and saving for the future as compared to the US, which strongly values consumption and living in the present.

It is very often that a career an individual chooses for himself/ herself is influenced by early communications received and imbibed from the family and society. And very often it is in keeping with the mindset of a secure job and income, or which is viewed positively by the society. Besides, family's occupational background also impacts the preferences of individuals towards becoming entrepreneurs. Thus, decisions are often relied to come from others, out of respect, a value strongly upheld by Indians. Often decisions taken by others are adhered to out of the habit of doing what is told rather than thinking about what to do, a way brought about from early years in education where it is ingrained in individuals to just follow instructions. Career decisions are based primarily on parental expectations first. Engineering and medicine have long been considered elite jobs in India, with many parents wanting their children to become one of them. Children often accept the decisions their parents take for them, sometimes even when they may have other aspirations. This is partly due to the habit of not questioning and challenging imbibed from early years in schooling and later on in the job environments. This leads to inability to cultivate an attitude of innovation and original thinking. Besides, social pressures of getting married and settling down in a family often comes in the way of a career's progress, especially in the case of women. There is a general inclination to work less and have a pressure free life with the needs being few.

Sometimes, the demography of a country also influences people's choice of career. This influence may arise due to historical factors of insecurity or peace, or extent of enrichment from natural resources. For example, the western and southern regions in India are more entrepreneurially active than the eastern regions. And that is why, many IT firms were set up down south and a plethora of south Indians constituted the Indian Diaspora.

The nature of governance and policies enacted also affects the business culture of a country. While the U.S still has many bureaucratic, paternal organizations, it is swiftly moving in the direction of flatter, participatory corporations. India's culture, on the other hand, supports strong hierarchical organizations and autocratic superiors. It has been observed that professionals in India believe that trust and ethics are less important than pleasing customers. The Satyam saga is a case in point. Satyam was one of the top IT companies in India but was found conducting unethical business practices, which ultimately led to its doom and a tainted image for the Indian IT industry. The companies however, counter this observance by stating that the poor ethics in Indian companies is a result of systemic corruption where poor implementation of laws is to blame for unethical business practices. While much has been touted about the benefits of doing business in India -- low input costs, easy access to labor and a massive consumer base, the grimmer side of Indian companies' ability to thrive by bending rules, greasing palms and broadening ethical boundaries has not gone unnoticed. A unsatisfactory legal framework and regulatory mechanism, rigid bureaucracy, various ground-level hassles and lots of procedural delays are a serious concern, often resulting in lax ethical standards. Often companies resort to 'jugaad', which refers to the spirit of innovation in Indians to get the work completed and achieve end result through whatever means necessary and forms the backbone of the Indian growth story. Over the years, efforts have been made to smoothen procedures and strengthen mechanisms, including a drastic reduction in bureaucratic interferences and controls resulting from a rising awareness to harness the India competitive advantage. Even the high and mighty have faced jail and corruption charges which was impossible to even think about a few decades back. This change is in turn helping in a better investment climate, but even then, a lot more needs to be done at lower levels.

India's workforce is preponderantly young with large numbers entering the professional workforce every year. But access to professional education, socialization, entry and career advancement is still disproportionately concentrated among social groups that have traditionally dominated the professional fields. Despite its many strengths, the educational system doesn't provide sufficient trained talent for the job market, particularly the IT sector. This puts special pressures on employers in India for finding and competing for or holding and cultivating the skilled employees required. The legal safeguards, redress mechanisms and monitoring processes in India are also less developed. Discrimination in recruitment, selection and career advancement are less likely to be aggressively challenged.

Issues with the current model of outsourcing

The rapid growth of the IT industry over the last 20 years has had a good effect on the economic development across the world and India has emerged as a significant nation in the global IT space especially for IT services offshoring, catering to numerous companies of the world. IT outsourcing and offshoring has become a key source of increased export earnings, an important driver for the transformation of the domestic economy and an international interface for many Asian economies. The main thrust from India in the development of IT has been wholly in the area of outsourcing, where it held the advantage of having skilled labor available at a much lower cost than many developed nations. Along with this, advancements in communication technology, adequate infrastructure development, a maturing software industry and valuable international reputation acquired over the last 15 years have contributed to India's shift towards outsourcing. However, the Indian information technology outsourcing and offshoring is now facing continuously increasing problems of people, economy and government, thereby losing its competitive edge in the global race for IT supremacy. Slowing economy in the US has forced companies of all sizes to review their IT spending and demand from their vendors, mostly present in India, to become more flexible. New payment models involving spending in the form of operating expenditures and payment on-demand usage are being propagated by many. Due to growing anti-offshoring sentiments in the wake of the global slowdown, many countries are resorting to protectionism and are discouraging outsourcing and offshoring of their work to other nations.

In recent times, India is not faring well in terms of skilled labor output, one of the chief requirements for an outsourced country. Low worker performance standards has resulted in outsourcing nations losing trust in India's potential and they are now even looking at other markets as alternatives. This in turn has increased competition from IT outsourcing firms in China, Eastern Europe, Russia, Philippines, Vietnam and Middle East.

India has been struggling to keep up with increasing inflation rates over the last few years. Infrastructural bottlenecks have started to plague the outsourcing industry. With salaries of the workforce soaring to new heights, the cost arbitrage capacity, one of the most important elements in offshoring, will be reducing. But while, the salaries have gone significantly higher in the last 15 years, the billing rates have remained restrained in comparison. The operational cost is transferred to the customers, who are now denying to share the burden. Moreover, even Indian IT firms, which follow a pyramid model, wherein low cost, fresh graduates are hired every year to deliver projects at a good profit margin, are now reeling under pressure of rising salaries.

Political and bureaucratic corruption in India has been a major concern since many years. It has been found in a business survey, conducted across 12 economies, that India's civil servants are the least efficient among their Asian peers, describing them as "slow and painful" and making the Indian bureaucracy "suffocating". Moreover, multi-party rule results in very slow policy decision making and impacting any new initiatives.

Many global IT companies, having had a good experience with outsourcing to India and having built confidence in the local environment, are now setting up their own local subsidiaries in India. Companies such as Intel, Accenture, Cisco, IBM, have their workforce in India, with majority of their work operations executed from India. Thus, with captive models of business becoming popular, loss of revenue and high competition for talent is rising from within. Since the beginning of the IT industry in India, the primary growth engines for the Indian outsourcing industry has been the Time & Material and Fixed Price business models coupled with onshore and offshore models. These models of business will sooner or later become redundant, especially as IT services are moving higher up the value chain towards innovation process outsourcing.

Indians companies have not spent enough effort to come up with significant innovations in self-developed products or in business models. One of the main reasons India has not yet realized its full potential in innovation is because of the inability of the education system to inculcate a spirit of innovation, questioning and exchange of free ideas. This calls for an urgent change in the education system to make it promote experiments and innovation, along with promotion of stronger competition among enterprises, commercialization of new knowledge and fostering research and development activities even for the grass-root enterprises. Moreover, India lacks a product ecosystem compared to the encouraging environment of the US Silicon Valley. When commencing operations, Indian IT firms lacked access to risk capital required for product start-ups and a reasonable understanding of the market. So they utilized the large workforce and low cost advantage to build companies based on offshoring models of business. However, after several years of successfully conducting business, these firms have gained the much required knowledge and have built their own financial strength to self-fund. Hence, they should now shift their focus towards building their own product portfolio.

Besides, these grave challenges, there are other negligible ones like Data Security, currency fluctuations, quality of service and cultural issues that the Indian IT industry is facing currently.

Change is needed

The Indian IT industry has now completed one full lifecycle, through which it has witnessed rapid growth and development, but is now plagued by multiple challenges. The IT industry by definition is all about innovation and the only constant in this industry is change. Thus, these challenges present before the IT business model followed by India for more than 25 years now, is nothing more than a standard change process where one form gives way to another and change keeps happening. However, while some companies have realized that the next wave of change is here, many IT companies are still living in fool's paradise, ignoring warning signals and managing these issues by mere salary cuts or even hiring even more substandard work force at lower costs.

IT employees in India have been a pampered lot but are now staring at a not so bright future. After almost a free run since the last two decades barring brief periods during dot com bust and 2007 recession, most mid and small scale companies are now struggling to keep employees ranks intact and have been plagued by an average 25% attrition rate. While Indian employment environment was not created to hire and fire, this culture of pink slips are becoming common place with several large companies apart from small ones resorting to cuts in work force. Salary increase freeze or low increase as compared to previous years is becoming common. This shakeup is part of the change cycle and is inevitable. Almost all companies have experienced more challenges in their businesses than ever before. Many have seen customers exiting due to reasons like budget cuts, getting a better deal or even opting out for their own captive company in India.

Though India is the largest IT services provider, it has absolutely no credible intellectual property even after 25 years of experience and even after having all the conducive factors and great opportunities. The short-sighted approach of Indian IT leaders has led them to grab the quick fixes easy money options as a result of which, body shopping has gone farther than what was reasonable.

Traditional body shopping models are already being challenged when they are compared with a better run captive setup where getting 50% cost benefit is normal. Indian IT industry has bet rather too much on body shopping than what should have been. With time virtually running out, there are no leaders in sight who could show the way forward for India in creating the likes of Google and Apple in India.

With problems aplenty, the Indian IT needs an overhauling right from the grass-roots level to be able to embark on the next wave of change. There is a need for the country to transform the general culture of work, ethics, business and development, to its education system, and an urgent need for an image makeover. The time to "fill in for gaps" is being fast replaced with a time demanding "innovation and creation". However, for this to happen, the citizens need to move away from their "settled mind-set" to one encouraging creation of new products. Risk taking capacity needs to increase, along with creation of a conducive environment for growth of entrepreneurship. New ventures should be provided a growth impetus through proper nurturing of talent, valuable mentoring and adequate funding from investors. Capital investors need to shift focus from merely reaping profits and assured returns on their investments to encouraging free thought and out of the box creations. An approach to building new innovation ecosystems supplemented by embracing new technologies, scaling education and bridging relationships between investors, entrepreneurs and companies to channel the flow of talent, information and financial resources in the direction of constant evolution is the need of the hour.

The uncertain and complex challenges of the new era requires workers to work with different ethos and economic situations. To combat the difficult economic conditions, more focus needs to be put in nurturing entrepreneurship as a way to kick-start the economy and create new high-growth ventures to further create wealth and employment. Industry and society should encourage entrepreneurs and the education system should support this thought process. Great institutes like IIM should focus their training in producing world class entrepreneurs instead of highly paid job seekers. Industry should extend their CSR (Corporate social responsibilities) in helping budding entrepreneurs to be nurtured and established. There is a great need for managers who can operate across cultural differences with an entrepreneurial and global mindset.

For the preservation of the nation's competitiveness and economic opportunities in response to rapid technological changes and increasing global competition, a constant requirement of highly skilled workforce is essential for which education should be partnered with industry. Such an education-industry partnership can play a unique role in providing the academic and applied learning that satisfies the demand for skilled employees and the need for a knowledgeable and an engaged citizenry. Partners can contribute human resources, finances, facilities and equipment and leadership acumen to help align education with the new challenges of business demands and generate a workforce well equipped with trending knowledge.

With the world getting flatter, knowledge economy is developing on a global scale, driven and magnified by communications, transport and IT revolutions.

This requires development of an effective ecosystem for a globally integrated workforce in India, for a diverse mix of talented employees across educational levels and professional skills categories. This will bring about trans-border skills networks, open access to global labs for innovation, leveraging collective intelligence from diverse employees and customers, new platforms for value creation, cost and quality integration with innovation and globalization of R&D for breakthrough outcomes. India needs to shed its hierarchal corporate image, create a culture for creativity, reduce government-created bottlenecks, usher in stringent rules for IPR and national security.

With the recent report released by the Hong Kong- based Political & Economic Risk Consultancy Ltd. that Indian bureaucracy is the worst in Asia with a 9.21 rating out of 10, an image makeover takes on a new urgency. India's inefficient and slow bureaucracy is the single largest complaint by business executives. A desperate improvement drive to remove the tainted image and build a new brand of credibility, innovation and a land of growth and opportunity should be the top priority as the country takes on the new wave. This calls for more stringent government guidelines and public vigilances, removal of the government's position as autonomous, identifying key measures related to good governance along with a monitoring mechanism to track implementation. Moreover, Indian IT companies can benefit greatly from an image makeover in the United States too, by creating jobs there instead of being simply known as a third world dump for US firms shipping work overseas to take advantage of cheap labour. This can effectively happen when India is also able to showcase high quality work, which will help bring talents from across the world. India can become a large provider of jobs to US and European citizens in India. Investment by companies in these countries will help create local jobs too.

The Indian IT professionals need to start adjusting to a new normal where the mantra will be to perform or perish. Days of hefty pay hikes will be replaced with satisfaction of retaining jobs. The Indian government and every IT leader needs to move up the value chain from basic data entry and technology work to harnessing the real intellectual power of Indians. The focus of the IT sector should now be on retaining the customer rather than acquiring new customers. It would not work well for companies to continue luring customers into doing business by passing discounts or doing a lot of free work or even pay per use model to mitigate the risks. It will only end up in lower cash flow and higher cost of retaining the customer and further straining profits.

Companies are not taking advantage of knowledge earned in developing intellectual properties but focusing more on making profit by pushing body shopping business, which will vanish with time. Instead of creating a research and development environment, lots of energy is wasted in creating millions of commodity skills which will not be required with changing times.

F O U R
GLOBAL CHANGING SCENARIO

Year 2012 marks a landmark year for the Indian IT-BPO sector as aggregate revenues is expected to exceed $100 billion and when compared to a figure of a mere half billion dollar 20 years ago, this is a laudable achievement. The sector provides livelihood to 10 million people (including 2.8 million directly employed) and is the largest recruiter in the organized private sector. It is also amongst the biggest foreign exchange earners for the country with exports pegged at USD 69 billion for FY2012.

While figures conveying the outstanding success of this sector on one hand, the qualitative impact from the industry is even more outstanding. It has transformed the global image of India and Indians by showcasing their capabilities and portraying India as a land for business opportunities. It has energized the country's higher education sector, especially in engineering and computer science, and has subsequently provided for lucrative job avenues to thousands from even small towns and villages, and promoted gender equality by extensively employing women. It has raised hopes of many young people, who can view a future of growth and opportunity with optimism.

Technology has always taken the world by surprise, from bringing about an industrial revolution, to multitude of economic changes as well as social transformations. Like any other technology, Information Technology is no exception and as its evolution, advancements and results continue to spread at a rapid pace, so does humanity's dependence on it. As such, technology can never perish, only change form. And probably this is the reason why despite global uncertainties and low consumer confidence in 2011, global spending on technology continued unabated and demand for global sourcing for IT-BPO services remained strong.

Outsourcing sector in India too, has withstood all speculations and outcries and has prevailed as a viable business model for global industries. It began during the Y2K crisis and the dot com boom, with later the setbacks of recession demanding organizations to develop business strategies better aligned with market realities, and has now, post recessionary phase, emerged as an important strategic tool rather than a reactive decision to measure the ever changing business dynamics. Organizations continue to flock around locations focusing on lowering their operational costs. Even with stiff competition from other new locations for outsourcing, India retains its position as the world's leading global sourcing destination for IT-BPO services with a share of 58 per cent in 2011.

However, the industry has not remained unbound by turbulent times and challenges that it faces now, and as a new wave of change sweeps through the sector, it casts doubts on the existing practices over their ability to survive. Measures have been initiated by western economies to prevent jobs from flowing out of their countries to destinations like India, with many now raising anti-outsourcing voices and promoting protectionist policies, and this is going to weigh heavily on the Indian IT-BPO industry. Stringent new visa norms are making it more challenging for the industry players to serve their customers in their biggest markets, especially the US, which has imposed a steep hike in the visa fees for the work permits for skilled workers, making it difficult for some of the IT resources to visit US for work. Competition between vendors has increased due to limited spending by clients in a recessionary environment. This has led to undercutting of prices to win a bid causing pricing pressures as contracts are won based on lowest price bids. Increased cost pressures are in turn affecting the margins of the companies. Clients are opting for new low-cost destinations like Philippines, Eastern Europe and Latin America, where they could get the similar cost advantage for utilization of skilled labor. This is adding to the already existing competitive environment since customers now have a choice of destination, which was by default India in the past. Clients have become more mature when it comes to outsourcing, with better controls in place, not just to manage outsourcing but also to measure the quality of delivered goods. So with their expectations high, they now demand more from vendors, but this has not been coupled with increased spending. And with the slower than expected economic recovery, companies are taking precautionary measures by decreasing spending and investments, impacting the order pipeline of IT companies in India and delaying contract closures. Top Indian players have managed to position themselves globally and proved their cutting edge solutions across verticals and functions, but are till now looked upon as mere vendors instead of partners. They allow only limited or no access to boardroom decisions. Indian software industry is plagued with weak patent protection and high piracy.

There is an urgent need for the government to put in place a strong IP protection law after evaluating if the current IP laws and judicial systems are geared up to handle cases of complex dimensions that are likely to arise in the future with advancing technology and innovations.

Thus, the Indian IT-BPO industry today stands at an inflection point in its evolution. The remarkable progress exhibited by the Indian IT-BPO industry in the past may not have a free run for long as the future brings increasing complexity. Business leaders are agreeing that the next decade will be substantially different from the previous one, in which new business models will emerge to deal with a rapidly changing marketplace and customer needs.

Outsourcing is currently transforming from the existing service provider-client model to a productive partnership model that promises to bring in industry expertise, process excellence and strong delivery capability, further adding to the organization's overall growth.

With the outsourcing industry getting mature and service providers and clients aiming to establish long term relationships in business, cost saving is no more a dominant factor for outsourcing. These trends in outsourcing are gradually changing and the traditional model of outsourcing is now being replaced with a global sourcing model where quality resources matching the client's specific objectives are selectively sourced from global destinations.

Another emerging trend in outsourcing industry is 'captives' where the offshore center acts as a natural extension or Global in-house center for the client. Such new models are promising a cost saving of almost 40-70 percent and adding to the capabilities of the parent organization. The social layer, which has spread itself atop almost every consumer-related service, is now spreading fast into enterprise space. Companies are now interacting with their customers directly through various mediums not confined to the traditional channels. So now when creating business tools or various enterprise applications, IT vendors need to think about social interactions right from the inception. In the past 3-4 years, consumer has seen the growing use of 'Smartphones' and more recently 'Tablets', which have added to mobility of technology - the underlying principal to the rapid expansion of these new product types. IT/technology vendors and clients will need to think 'Mobile up' design strategies rather than create a solution and then make it mobile enabled. With ways of communication transforming and evolving, IT vendors need to treat communication as a platform over which other experiences are built, and not vice versa. The consumers of today want to communicate from anywhere through any device or any application. While earlier, the 'market' for all the latest in technology used to be the west, an increased rate of technology adoption has put India abreast with new developments in the west. India is central to the global mobile and Internet revolution with the highest user penetration. This gives Indian technology firms an opportunity to use the domestic market as testing grounds for path breaking technologies and solutions like mobile workspace, mobile peer-to-peer payments, mobile banking, mobile shopping etc., before they take their solutions to global platforms. The ushering of the cloud computing age has led to more and more core services like SaaS (Software as a Service), RIM (Remote Infrastructure Management), etc., getting outsourced to centralized centers, thereby reducing the required infrastructure and manpower needed and bringing down the cost significantly. Thus, the trend in outsourcing will continue to change and the ability of businesses to quickly respond to market changes and keep pace with it will determine its success. At this critical juncture, firms need to look beyond the conventional linear growth models and turn to innovative non-linear forms of growth.

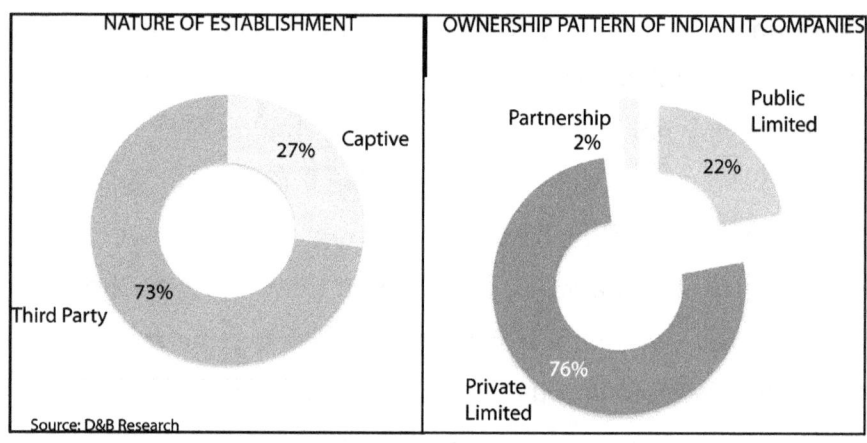

One of the key benefits India has as a major player for outsourcing is the cost advantage it offers to the clients. In fact, India ranks first among a host of desirable nations in terms of cost, which includes employee cost, infrastructure cost, management cost and the tax reliefs. However, this cost arbitrage is slowly abating and with it looms the fear of the industry becoming redundant. With labor cost increasing, burdening the overall cost of service and decreasing benefit for both the client and the service-provider, what then would be the need to outsource to India? Indian IT-BPO industry is facing numerous challenges in hiring, managing and retaining talent in the current environment. The industry, which is still in its nascent stage in India, is already experiencing a dearth of middle management level and senior managers. Entry-level recruitment and employment has not posed much of a problem with many fresh graduates, equipped with good language skills, readily available in the job market. However, the problem is more intense for the third-party outsourcing companies who have just ventured into this business. They lack the resources to invest in proper training and thus, poach middle and senior level managers from other companies. Though hiring from competitors is a cyclical process which will not help the industry grow, but with few options available, many companies resort to the easy solution - poaching. That leads to high attrition, which not only means loss of talent, but also includes the additional cost of training the new recruits. Of all the challenges faced by the BPO organizations at various levels, attrition, absenteeism and keeping the employees motivated are dominant at the middle level. The attrition rate in the IT-BPO industry has been hovering around 35%. An average Indian call center employee works with a company for 11 months, whereas an average UK call center employee stays in a company for 3 years. Despite potential for tremendous growth, BPO industry continues to suffer from high levels of attrition.

REASONS FOR ATTRITION

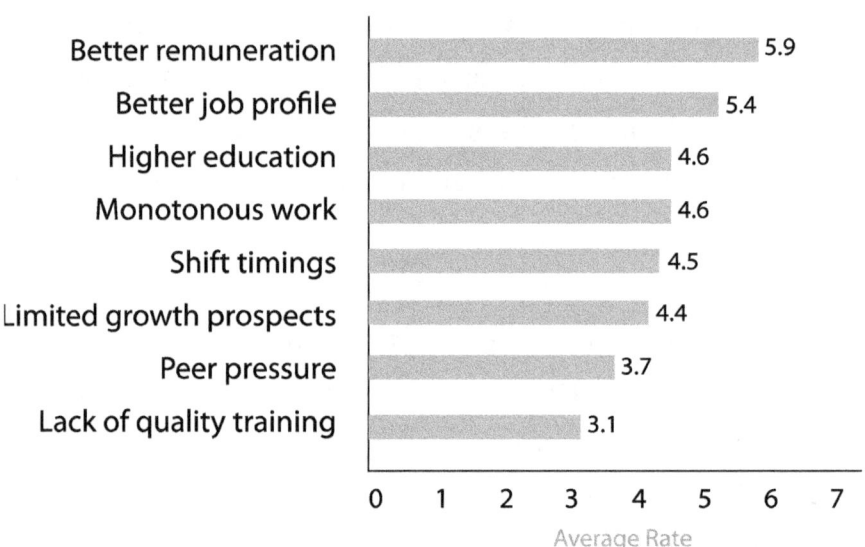

Source: D&B Research

Wage inflation is another important factor contributing to the reducing cost arbitrage. Today experienced employees are drawing almost 70 percent of US salary and given that even a junior employee is "experienced' in a short time, the number of people drawing high salaries in a company is nothing but additional cost burden to the vendors, defying the whole purpose of setting up shops in India 'for the vast talent pool that is not so inexpensive'. There is also the cost and startup inefficiencies of setting up a development unit on the other side of the world which can be significantly reduced with the help of experienced consultants, but getting the right advice is also not easy to find.

A sluggish GDP growth worldwide, FDI outflows and the economic turmoil, has had a dampening effect on the Indian rupee, which has been witnessing huge swings in recent months. While post 2011, the weakening of Indian rupee has brought some good news for exporters including software exporters like TCS and Infosys, high volatility has added to the woes of the IT-BPO industry. Most of the large IT companies resort to hedging of the dollar against Indian Rupee to offset any risk of negative fluctuation, but get impacted when fluctuation happens in positive side as they are unable to encash the benefit while expenses follow the inflation route. According to NASSCOM, even a 10% movement in the currency will definitely add to the concern of the BPO companies irrespective of its size. The volatility in currency poses a major challenge to the BPO firms since for the offshore work, they earn their revenues in dollars and the expenses have to be met in Indian rupees.

The huge employee base in Indian IT-BPO companies is more a problem now than asset as operational complexity increases along with increasing HR costs. Even with a large pool of graduating engineers, they stand largely unemployable due to deficiencies in the current system of education. This is becoming a recurrent cry in the IT-BPO sector, which is grappling with issues of not being able to recruit efficient employees. Since the industry-academia gap leaves companies no choice but to invest heavily in training, these training investments are being increasingly viewed as an additional cost.

Thus, these factors such as increasing attrition, wage inflation, skills shortages, operational complexity in managing large pool is making it difficult for IT-BPOs to work efficiently and promise the same cost arbitrage it once enjoyed. If the current cost arbitrage can be pegged at 40 percent of a US labor, then it may sustain for 17-20 years in a best case scenario, or 8-10 years in a worst case scenario as per a study done by Everest Consulting in 2011. High growth in this sector has resulted in a lot of inefficiencies, which has partially reduced the overall cost arbitrage advantage. Efficiently managed setups will continue to give attractive cost arbitrage for a very long time.

DISRUPTIVE TECHNOLOGIES

According to Clayton Christensen from Harvard business school, "A disruptive technology is a new technological innovation, product or service that eventually overturns the existing dominant technology or product in the market." Disruptive technologies create new markets, disrupt existing markets and value network or displace an earlier technology. Advent of disruptive technologies such as cloud computing are posing a threat to traditional IT outsourcing models by increasingly hosting IT infrastructure of enterprises – large, medium or small - in their own data centers, thereby reducing their IT costs significantly. Others such as SOA, big data, legacy modernization are all creating a different set of customers in the market, slowing the processes of existing markets, displacing earlier technology or greatly augmenting existing to create new value.

With challenges before IT service providers of shortening contracts, increased protectionism and various regulatory hurdles, linear growth—or growing by just adding employees —may not prove beneficial in the long run for many Indian and multinational IT firms. Tier-I Indian IT firms have more than 100,000 employees each and with wages rising by 10-12% annually, Indian IT firms will become less competitive in the next few years and the competition will only get tougher.

These new technologies are difficult to recognize and existing firms are more reluctant to incorporate them. Smaller companies are more accepting of disruptive technologies using it to target niche areas of the market or in order to make their company more attractive for acquisition.

New platforms brought about by disruptive technologies has the ability to break the traditional outsourcing models and bring about a change in the balance of delivery. Increasing popularity of non-linear technologies are forcing Indian IT companies to rethink their strategies and move up the value chain by also sharing financial and business risks with clients, moving to a more flexible outcome-based and output-based pricing rather than a fixed price model, and adding consultancy services to their portfolio, thus becoming partners in business. These disruptive trends present new opportunities in the form of largely untapped markets and new customer segments. However, these opportunities also bring along an added set of risks of increased protectionism and regulatory control from sourcing markets, and increased competition from new and emerging countries.

Cloud computing

Information technology today is shifting gears rather fast. Companies are constantly aiming to cut costs and retain maximum productivity, and are thus, moving fast towards cloud computing for shared infrastructure on pay per use basis. Cloud computing with its promise to bring about flexibility, scalability and cost benefits has stirred up interest and investments in many parts of the world. Replacing the rigid software and service licensing models in large, small and medium enterprises, cloud offers a prominent computing alternative today with utility based pay-per-use services, terabytes and gigabytes of storage at a very marginal cost and subscription to a suit of applications for just a few dollars per annum. Scalability, flexibility, virtualization and cost being the essential business drivers, cloud based on a production model is designed as a means to offer software application to end-users and bring about operational efficiency to providers. It offers software as a service – business operations over a network (eg -Cisco, Webex, Intuit); infrastructure as a service – rent, processing, storage; and platforms as a service – deploy customer-created application to a cloud (eg - Amazon Web services, Google App Engine).

Cloud computing offers:

1. SaaS

Software as a service offers a software delivery model through the browser, with the software and associated data located centrally on cloud. The hardware and software maintenance and support is taken care by the SaaS provider, sparing the customers from upfront investments in servers or software licensing. With just one application to maintain by the third party cloud service provider, costs are much lower compared to conventional hosting. SaaS is common for sales, HR, ERP and even "desktop" applications, such as Google Apps and Zoho Office.

2. Utility computing

Cloud computing as a form of utility computing offers storage and virtual servers that IT can access on demand. While utility computing is mainly used for supplemental, non-mission-critical needs currently, they may one day replace parts of the datacenter. Some provide solutions that help IT create virtual data-centers from commodity servers, such as 3Tera's AppLogic and Cohesive Flexible Technologies' Elastic Server on Demand, thus enabling IT to stitch memory, I/O, storage and computational capacity as a virtualized resource pool available over the network.

3. Web services on the cloud

Web service providers deviate from delivering full applications to offering APIs that enable developers to exploit functionality over the Internet. They range from providers offering distinct business services, such as Strike Iron and Xignite, to the full range of APIs such as those offered by Google Maps, ADP payroll processing.

4. Platform as a service

PaaS delivers a development environment as a service, allowing the customer to build their own applications and run them on the provider's infrastructure, which are delivered to users via the Internet from the provider's servers. The consumer controls the software deployment and configuration settings and the provider provides the networks, servers and storage capability.

5. MSP (managed service providers)

MSP offers applications exposed only to IT rather than to end-users, such as a virus scanning service for e-mail or an application monitoring service.

6. IaaS

One of the most basic cloud service model, IaaS providers offer computers – as physical or virtual machines, storage, firewalls, load balancers and networks. IaaS providers supply these resources on demand from their large pool installed in data centers.

Cloud helps drastically reduce cost as payment for cloud services is made incrementally, saving organizations huge sums of upfront cost. Instead of investing in high-powered workstations loaded with software, networking infrastructure and servers, cloud computing offers all of it on an offsite, secure environment, guaranteed by the cloud provider. With most of the hardware been taken off the budget, companies are rendered free from IT management, support and maintenance costs. Enterprises could scale resources and applications to meet the needs of customers and have the flexibility to efficiently commence and withdraw operations, which would not be possible otherwise, given the huge investments made. Moreover, organizations can store more data on cloud than on private computer systems. It is highly automated and not IT personnel dependent, thus doing away with the cost of large manpower and other resources. Cloud computing offers much more flexibility than past computing methods with access to information wherever an employee may be. It leaves IT with fewer worries about constant server updates and other computing issues. Besides, it offers security of backups that are more reliable and flexible in operations. The software runs in the host environment, from where the employees can securely and quickly access the company's data and software from anywhere with just an Internet connection. So even a small or mid-sized business owner or executive can now move towards reaping benefits of a cloud computing solution, which can bring about almost 20% or more in IT cost reductions.

Cloud computing operates in a shared environment by a third party provider who invests in the server grids and appliances, which are used by customer's end users. This ensures efficient utilization and management of applications, hardware and software and economies of scale by spreading infrastructure cost over many subscribers. Cloud caters to multiple customers through a single delivery platform, which makes it an attractive investment for the service providers because with an increase in customer base, the fixed cost incurred in creating and delivering services is recovered faster and over a long term, the service provider can register high profits himself. After the initial years of investment and cost incurred in sales, marketing, customer acquisition and customer churning, margins are likely to be phenomenal once revenue crosses a threshold.

Cloud computing offers a significant shift in the business and economic models for provisioning and consuming information technology (IT) through resource pooling that can lead to a significant cost savings. Thus, the cloud era in a way signals a new normal that calls forth low cost of IT by far more effective and efficient methods of operations along with ensuring effective utilization of investments. Cloud, public or company owned private clouds are giving far more effective infrastructure services than what was happening all along.

CLOUD COMPUTING CONSIDERATION FACTORS

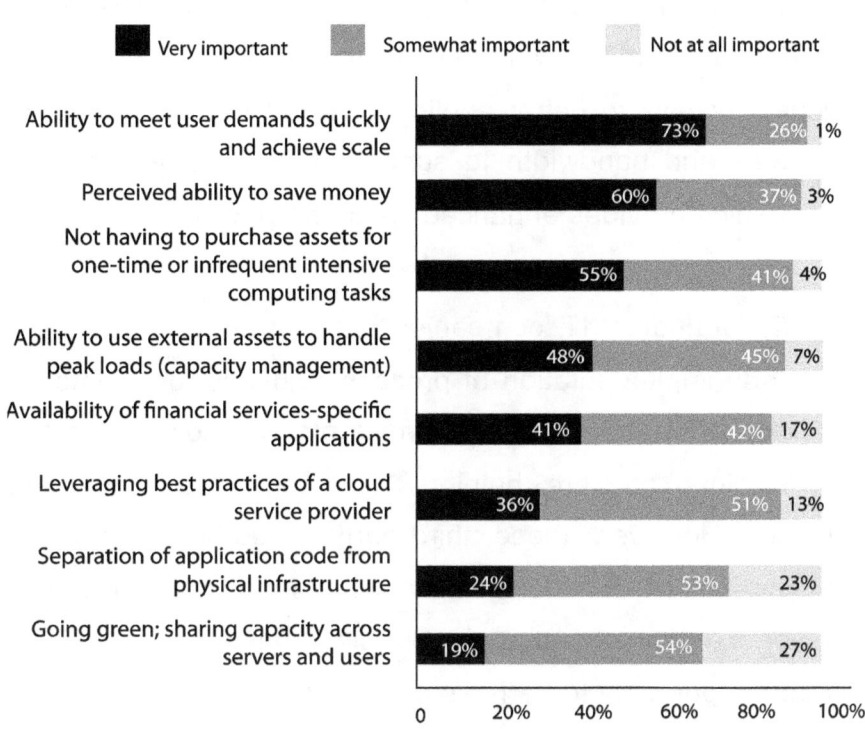

Source: InformationWeek Analytics/InformationWeek Financial Services
Cloud Computing Survey of 642 financial services technology professionals

Cloud is especially beneficial for small businesses and sole proprietorships as they can drastically reduce burden on IT budgets as all the equipments, servers and appliances are set up by a third party provider, also relieving them of large head-counts required to manage, as cloud takes care of maintenance. Cloud makes possible fast and flexible deployment of applications, which internal IT departments normally take months to deploy. Customers always have the option to expand or withdraw these services at any time. Besides, access to better applications that require additional resources and bandwidth to support them is taken care by cloud, which provides enhanced computer power.

Majority of Indian IT companies are currently engaged in third-party implementation of process solutions for clients on their cloud (e.g. enabling a business process solution on the client's cloud) or are helping implement cloud migration services. However, these third-party cloud-based process implementations are modest in revenues and are still part of traditional outsourcing models. But cloud offers Indian IT-BPO another opportunity to harness the new technology and take a leap in the global playing field and possibly emerge as a leader. The next couple of years, given the sheer speed of technological advancements, as cloud offerings mature in terms of features and functions, its market outreach will explode and almost overtake desktop offerings in many areas.

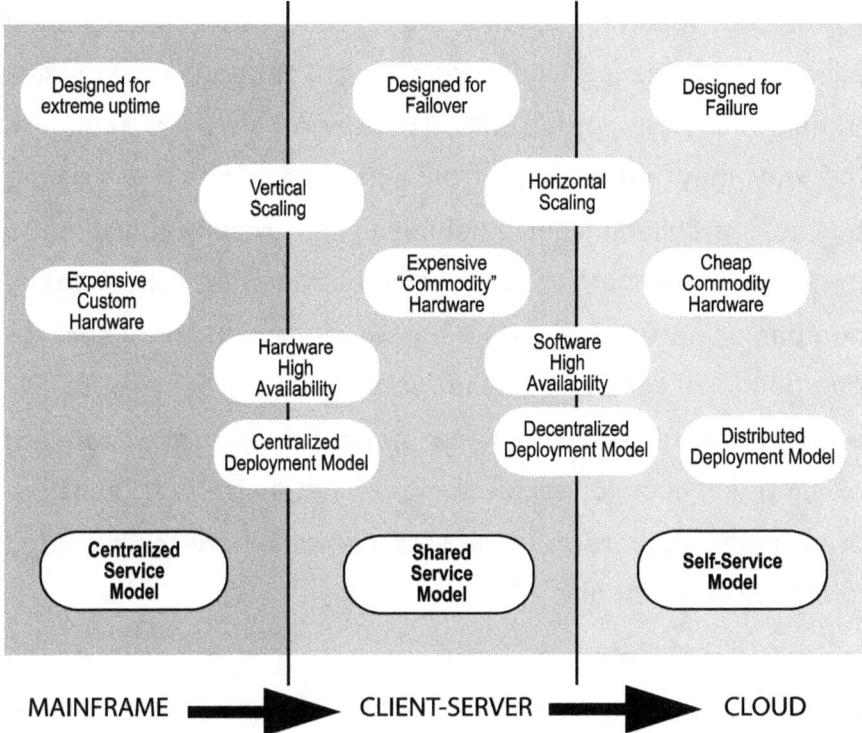

MAINFRAME ➡ CLIENT-SERVER ➡ CLOUD

Source: cloudhostingprovider.co.uk

SOA (Service-Oriented Architecture)

The business environment is changing gears fast calling for extensive simplification of information systems. Bloated information technology infrastructures of today are adding to process inefficiencies and offering no respite from the ever increasing recurring costs. But given the limited budget allocation to the service needs of an enterprise, extensive transformation is not feasible. There can only be a change in the way they are managed by either adding to the existing business architecture or by shuffling the existing functions to meet the changing customer requirements. Thus many companies are now adopting SOA, which provides an approach to restructure the service of an enterprise by eliminating redundancy and consolidating and reusing existing services for accelerating project delivery. All software of an enterprise are organized as software services provided internally or externally.

Service-oriented architecture allows management of usage (delivery, acquisition, consumption, and so on) in terms of related services, greatly impacting the management of software life cycle—right from specification of requirements as service, design of service, acquisition and outsourcing as a service, asset management as a service, and so on. It aims to allow users to string together large chunks of functionality to form ad hoc applications that are built almost entirely from existing software services, thereby creating the application at a fairly low cost as all of the software required to satisfy the requirements of the new application, already exists, hence requiring only the orchestration process to produce a new application.

Like objects and components, services are natural building blocks that combine information and behavior, hide internal workings from outside intrusion and present a relatively simple interface to the rest of the organization. Services provide high levels of adaptability through aspect or context orientation and can be published and consumed singly or as hierarchies and as collaborations.

SOA supports service discovery allowing a service consumer in need of a service to easily discover the service dynamically. This helps remove compile time dependencies and makes maintainability easier as consumers do not require a new interface binding every time the interface changes. SOA provides modularity of decomposition that allows for breaking of an application into smaller modules also referred to as 'top-down' design. It also provides modularity of composibility which allows for production of software services that can be combined freely as a whole with other services to generate new systems, also referred to as 'bottom-up' design. SOA encourages interoperability allowing for systems using different platforms and languages to communicate with each other. This can be successfully achieved by supporting the protocol and data formats of the service's clients, by mapping the characteristics and languages of each platform to a mediating specification. SOA should allow for loose coupling between service consumer and service provider through use of contracts and binding. A consumer enquires about a service through a third-party registry, which presents all the available services that match the criteria of the consumer. The consumer then chooses the service to use, binds to it and executes the method on it. Thus the consumer is not directly dependent on the service's implementation but only on the contract the service supports. Loose coupling allows for greater modification ease, as the more tightly coupled a system is, the more change in a service will be required. SOA must boast of a network addressable interface allowing a consumer on a network to invoke a service across a network and allowing service to be reused by any other consumer at any time. SOA needs to have a coarse-grained interface, as a service generally supports a single business process or concept, which can be reused in multiple large distributed systems. One of the key characteristics of SOA is its ability to offer location transparency, which keeps the service's location unknown unless located by the customer in the registry. This allows service implementation to move from location to location without the client's knowledge, thereby achieving greater availability and performance. Moreover, SOA has the ability to self heal from errors without human intervention during execution.

SOA (service oriented architecture) covers software as a service, platform as a service, Analytics as a service, infrastructure as a service and almost everything being done is now delivered to the customer in a pay per use model. It thereby reduces huge upfront costs associated with all these concepts. Through an integrated framework, different services are organized to work together and a common system governance framework is established to control operations. A well designed system can bring about better synchronization between business and IT implementation to move beyond alignment to consider convergence of business and IT processes. A well formed service provides a unit of management that relates to business usage. Enforced separation of the service provision helps understanding the life cycle costs of a service and how it is used in the business.

One of the key benefits of SOA adoption is business agility, making IT solutions rapidly adaptable to new and changing organizational requirements and strategies. SOA challenges the current model of man and material, which would not be enough to sustain business needs of future and will completely move to value-generation based model. The focus will shift from hourly cost to hourly value where IT service providers would look at deploying highly productive workforce and move away from headcount eventually.

SOA will enable companies develop new capabilities to aid in quickly responding to business changes thereby aligning business and IT more closely. The reuse of existing assets of an enterprise promotes increased efficiency with minimum cost, which would have otherwise incurred overhauling of process and transforming the service systems. IT systems are able to quickly leverage the readily available code bases and services from across organizations. Based on industry standards, SOA can reduce complexity as compared to integrating systems on a solution-by-solution basis. Future applications can be seamlessly meshed with existing services. It is simple and easy to maintain which inturn means reduced cost and reduced IT workforce. In fact, the multitudes of benefits that SOA provides ultimately allows companies to focus more resources on innovation and on delivering new business services.

In India adoption of SOA has been relatively slow, primarily because of lack of knowledge and misconceptions that SOA is more a technology requirement rather than a business decision. However, with the wave of change hitting hard, many enterprises are fast moving to SOA infrastructure - right from banking and financial services to manufacturing, retail, telecom, healthcare and even the government organizations are enquiring about SOA technology. India has been very successful in selling itself as a low-cost location with skills, and so maybe the next challenge could be to move India as the world's SOA center too.

Mobile Computing

The advent and subsequent surge of mobile devices, Smartphones and tablets has introduced the mobile computing era. This switch from desktop to mobile computing becomes official as shipments of smartphones and tablets surpass that of desktops and laptops. Increasing demand for internet-enabled devices has made communication through wireless technology much sought after. Mobile computing allows for use of computing capability without a pre-defined location and/or connection to a network to publish and/or subscribe to information. It enables human-computer interaction by means of making computing technologies highly portable. Today's fast paced world requires non-stop work for maintaining productivity for any business, organization or professional. While in the past, mobile computing was limited to notebook computers and similar hardware that allowed for physical portability of computer technologies, today, these are extended to non-bulky hardware such as mobiles, pads and PDAs with software and web solutions that bring the entire computing experience on hand held devices. Mobile data communication is a rapidly evolving technology allowing users to transmit data from remote locations to other remote or fixed locations, thus solving the problem of mobility. Supported by telecom providers through wireless broadband, mobile computing would change the way people use technology. Mobile computing technologies consists of three aspects - portable hardware, mobile software and mobile communication. Mobile hardware deals with the devices that are used for portable computing such as handsets, components, etc. Mobile software provides mobile applications and programs, which enable the hardware to function in a non-fixed environment. Mobile communication provides network and communication infrastructure, data format, protocols, etc.

Mobile computing makes possible to carry the virtual world wherever one is. There is no need to stay in one location for performing computing activities. Mobile computing gives unprecedented flexibility to move about and perform computing activities at the same time. Increased work flexibility brings about enhanced work productivity. Work can be carried out from any place, without waiting for or making efforts to get access to computing facilities, thereby leading to more work being done with greater flexibility. It facilitates data sharing and collaboration between users and allows them to stay digitally connected from any location. One of the most prominent cost cutting exercises for large organizations aiming at reducing costs involves reducing people and premises. One of the ways that companies can benefit from is to reduce regional offices and allow the staff to work from home, which is possible through mobile computing technologies. With Broadband speeds becoming faster, Wi-Fi hotspots becoming popular and enhanced communications bringing with it easy transferring of data, mobile video calling and video conferencing has become very easy.

Mobile computing looks more promising with simultaneous advancements in Artificial intelligence, Integrated Circuitry and increased processing speed. As enterprises adopt maturing technologies, more and more services are becoming available online without actual intervention of the service provider. Today there are over 840 million active mobile subscribers with almost 15 million mobile subscribers added every month. Banking, manufacturing and retail are leading the way in applying mobility service to their operations.

There is an urgent requirement for companies now to interact with customers directly through various mediums and this needs to be borne in mind by IT vendors while creating business tools and enterprise applications to integrate for cross platform mobile coverage. The growth of business would no longer be limited to phone calls and net browsing on such converged devices but would extend to conducting live business globally anywhere, anytime and with ultimate flexibility. From live telecast and TV channels, video conferencing, online data storage and almost all other facility can be done on the move today. This migration holds the key for a revenue stream for business models of tomorrow. Eventually, all computing devices and phones would now merge into a single unit providing immense flexibility to the end-user. Mobile computing will also allow users to work from home, with access to employees' workspace in offices from anywhere, adding mobility in business process along with eliminating transportation and other infrastructure costs.

Big Data & Data engineering

With surmounting data, fueled by the increasing information captured by enterprises and popularity of multimedia and social media, the key to harnessing the new wave of productive growth, innovation and consumer surplus will be by analyzing large data – or big data. "Big data" is datasets of enormous size and beyond the ability of typical database software tools to capture, store, manage and analyze data. Today, data is accumulating from all directions in extremely large numbers. Be it transactional data collected by

companies informing about customers, suppliers, operations, data from embedded network servers from mobile phones, automobiles etc, or be it data contributors from social media, smartphones, PCs, laptops - a large trail of data is being constantly created. Be it any sector, any economy, any organization and any user of digital technology, digital data is omnipresent.

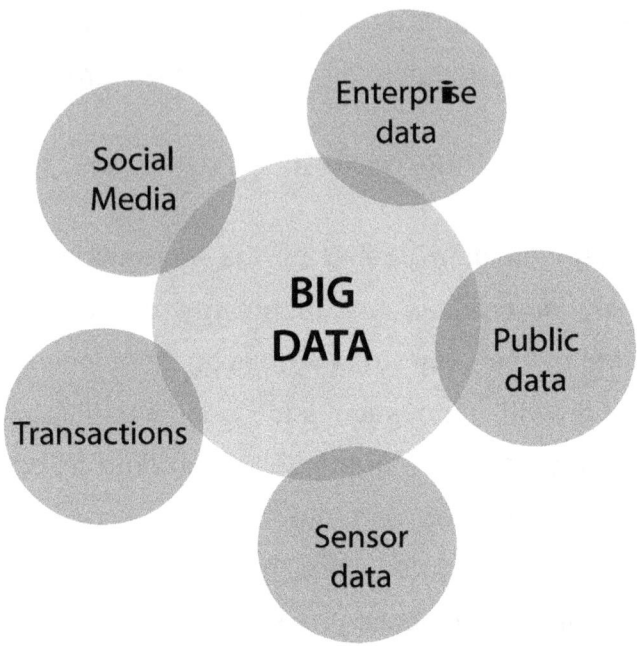

Big data is valuable in almost all sectors from healthcare, retail to manufacturing and even the public domain. Established companies and new entrants can leverage data-driven strategies to create value from information and innovate and compete alongside. Information will become transparent and usable at a greater frequency. As organizations create and store more data in digitized form, access to accurate and detailed information is easily possible, which in turn will increase productivity. Narrow segmentation of customers will help enterprises target customer needs more precisely, leading to creation of tailor made products and services. Customers would expect businesses they deal with to understand and proactively reach out to them for their needs.

Easy accessibility of big data to relevant stakeholders can add to value generation as timely availability of data can reduce time to market and improve quality. For example, if data is easy available across separate departments in a public sector organization, a lot of searching and processing time can be spared. Big data can provide organizations with accurate and detailed performance data on everything from product inventories to number of holidays taken by an employee. Variability in performance can be analyzed to help leaders manage performance to higher levels. Highly specific segmented information can be used by organizations to tailor products and services as per the need of each segment and market and promote accordingly. Decision-making will substantially improve with sophisticated data analytics and it will no longer be limited to the macro level but would permeate to individual levels. Marketing would become more focused and targeted through knowledge of past buying patterns and sentiments recorded in data. Big data can be utilized to improve the next generation of products and services. Based on data analysis, companies can create new products accordingly, enhance existing ones or invent new business models. Manufacturers are using big data obtained from utilization of their products to improve the development of the next generation of products, and even devising innovative after-sales offerings. Thus big data can encourage innovative products and approaches, help map a customer's need effectively and improve value, performance and efficiency of an organization in any sector. Big data will create new types of companies and various growth opportunities. For example, new companies to accumulate and analyze industry data will be set up, thus generating new sources of value and employment opportunities. Big data has the possibility of becoming a key basis of competition, underpinning new waves of productivity growth, innovation and consumer surplus.

So this mashing and processing of terabytes of data requires a plethora of infrastructure requirements, licenses and high cost, and is now easily and financially viable through commoditized hardware, cloud computing and open source software. This has made possible for small and big businesses alike to parcel the magnitude of data challenging established players. While earlier Indian IT service providers focused on providing value to the IT department of their clients, today they need to offer value to their end clients.

However, to realize the full potential of big data, issues related to privacy, security and intellectual property need to be adequately addressed. Right from the skilled workforce to structuring workflows and incentives to optimize the use of big data need to be worked out properly. For big data to be a success, access to data is critical and companies will need to increasingly integrate information from multiple data sources, often from third parties. Proper incentives need to be made to enable the free integration of data. India can take advantage of the growing demand for data analysts and managers by imparting training and education in data and analytical skills and management.

Today the possibility of storing, aggregating and combining data and then deeply analyzing this data is fast becoming popular and necessary for organizations in every sector. Big data is enabling a tremendous wave of innovation, productivity, growth, new modes of competition and value capture. Many companies are already using big data to create value. Government organizations can also boost efficiency and productivity significantly through the effective use of big data. Big data has reached every sector in the global economy and like the other essential factors of production such as hard assets and human capital, much of organization's economic activity is becoming more and more dependent on big data. The technologies used for Big Data like Hadoop have seen rapid adoption over last two years and it has potential to displace the traditional Data-warehousing through its visible and cost effective benefits over traditional licensed and layered data systems.

Legacy Modernization as a service

It has been observed that more than technology, business logic has brought about immerses value to companies. Today the priority of top management is to align business and IT goals. But it is here that legacy hardware and software come in the way of modernization. Many companies are running systems that are obsolete, slow and inflexible, which are like roadblocks to achieving optimum operational efficiency and deployment of new products. Much of the IT budget is dedicated to simply maintaining existing systems, rather than investing in new systems, making it more difficult to innovate and align IT and business effectively. Strategic alignment is only possible if maintenance cost is reduced and channelized towards investments in new projects.

Over the years, mainframe cost has substantially dropped but even then, customers feel that the price is too high and third-party software cost is a major inhibitor to the growth of mainframe. Along with high cost, there is also the growing problem of shrinking talent with mainframe technology skills, as now most universities do not offer mainframe education. Thus, this posses a challenge in the future to acquire personnel with mainframe skills. They would only become more difficult and expensive to get. Moreover, with focus on maintenance rather than productivity, innovation takes a back seat. Old legacy systems require high maintenance and companies spend almost 75 percent of their resources in maintenance, leaving little for innovations. If the maintenance cost is reduced to 33 percent, it would double the capacity of a company to innovate. There is an urgent need to move to a modern development environment to improve developer productivity. Many existing mainframe applications are difficult to enhance and adapt to current business practices due to their complexity and even a minute shift can disrupt the entire system. For innovation generation, the development cycle needs to accelerate and applications need to become flexible.

Continuation of legacy systems deters companies moving forward to cloud. Thus, the need to switch to contemporary platforms today is probably as important as technology itself. However, with companies now on cost saving mode and against the background of a shaky economic climate, they are forced to think twice before spending resources, be it even for the urgent need for modernization. Already, a lot of resources and time has been invested in creating robust IT systems over years. Over years, CIOs have started admitting that modernization is necessary for their survival and growth and the only little flexibility exists in the timing and the effective know-how of doing this exercise.

An approach towards modernizing legacy systems should be to evolve existing software and hardware to high performance assets by upgrading to latest versions, replacing old IT systems with advanced packages or redesigning for greater output. And this modernization of legacy system can be achieved at optimum cost, time and manpower resources, otherwise required to start from scratch and build new systems. The challenge before companies now is to set effective economic measures, but at the same time optimize business performance. And this requires aligning IT with business practices to improvise business standards, keeping it at zenith, and yielding effective IT performance.

MODERNIZATION STRATEGY

Modernization strategy offers choices of application replacement, application migration, application redevelopment and application integration. Application integration is an integral part of migration, replacement and redevelopment. So if the application is insufficient in serving the business needs, it can be migrated to new low cost platforms or replaced with a packaged offering. Modernizing legacy systems can down-size the maintenance cost to a great degree. Legacy systems resist change in business processes and coupled with lack of process orientation across organizations, they end up strangulating cost, production and performance. Modernized legacy systems, on the other hand, will be better equipped to adapt to changing business processes and strategically align IT with business. It will accord greater flexibility to alter or modify business processes at any strategic point. Modernization through an integration approach – be it migration, redevelopment or replacement or a combination of the three – can help create a more agile development environment.

Thus, modernizing legacy systems through up-gradation, replacement, redesign or migration will drastically reduce TCO, bring in a better and faster return on investment, increase profits, improve business standards and optimize production and operational efficiency. New business models would emerge to move these platforms from legacy to modern as a service to reap the best advantages of technological advancements over time. This will, in turn, automate a lot of work, which essentially would not require large number of IT professionals as it does today.

Social media

From profoundly changing the way we network, interact and find information, social media is fast maturing into a business model to generate economic returns. It will no longer be a mere platform for sharing and having fun, but indulge into business money transactions, gaming and more through an integration of social and business platforms.

Traditional working practices of operating in silos, with lack of collaboration or sharing of ideas and information across countries and even departments within an organization, are being challenged by new tools of social media that help connect easily and enable collaborative online working, disrupting the old ways of working. There is a growing acceptance of social media tools being more than distractions, but rather tools that could enable higher productivity and improved output.

Companies today are expanding to different geographical locations and remote working is a fast catching up trend, accelerating the need for greater cross-border collaboration and information sharing. The growth of business has to rely a great deal on the ability to collaborate thoughts and ideas from team members across various locations, collect relevant data and information quickly and rope in expertise and talent across the globe.

Though social media tools are not solely responsible for transforming business performance, they do most certainly possess great potential to augment businesses and drive future growth, if utilized appropriately. Challenging the existing silos and breaking down barriers of locations, adoption of social media tools is a must for business to survive. Such is the pace of digital revolution that almost 46 percent professionals feel the need for greater utilization of social tools for work. Many are using external social media such as Google+, Facebook, Twitter and LinkedIn for work purposes.

One of the chief benefits of using social media is its ability to make the flow of information and communication easy and better, thereby leading to improved cooperation between workers scattered across locations. It facilitates collection of ideas and thoughts, better collaboration and knowledge sharing, which has substantially enhanced professional relationships. Communication is the key process involved in various IT service management, such as change management, problem management, etc. Changes to the IT infrastructure are also dependent on good communication to manage user expectations and understand effects of changes on a day-to-day basis. Organizations using social media to support service management are able to solve problems faster and have also experienced a reduction in the level of frustration experienced by "uninformed" users.   Even with problem management, finding the causes for repetitive problems is easier with a good line of communication established between different areas of IT and between IT and its users. This will enable analysts to track recurring patterns over a much wider area than would otherwise be possible. Social media tools such as Twitter can help build strong rapport between the user community and service managers, and allow users to "self serve" or share experiences to find their own solutions.

The main purpose of any enterprise is understanding and satisfying its customer needs. Social media offers a chance to integrate the customer into the product or service, thus enabling customer to contribute to value creation. For example, Amazon.com allows buyers to review and discuss products. And this leads to improved value propositions based on customer inputs. Social media is transforming the way companies market their products and service. As customers now rely more on friends and peers to influence their buying decisions, and not on company marketing, here social media can focus on existing customers as channels to reach out to friends and peers. Social media can also boost open innovation by making it possible to transcend organizational boundaries. Social media will become a large platform for generating productive value out of workforce channelizing their time, intelligence and energy to do things that will have a direct impact on participating businesses.

SOCIAL MEDIA ROI

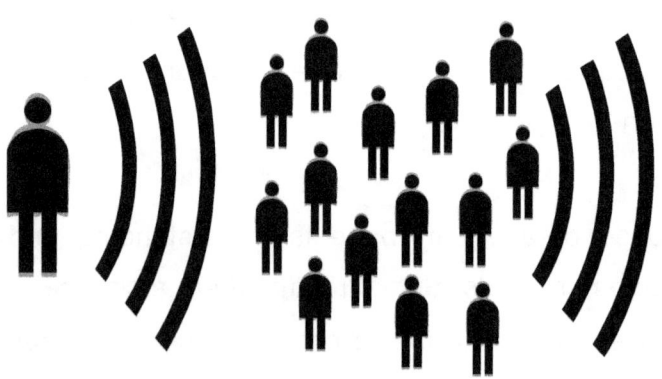

Efficiency
Reputation
Differentiation
Risk Reduction
Client Retention
Brand Association
Long Term Revenue
Environmental Impact
Economic Development
Opportunity Creation
Immediate Revenue
Perception Shifting
PR and Exposure
Client Education
Network Growth
Building Trust
Innovation

Source: Social Roi^{tm} Shane Gibson

Social media is used greatly to find people and expertise, widen personal network, build profiles and communities and professional relationships from a geographically dispersed team. Professionals using social tools have witnessed significant impact on the growth of organizations, increase in sales and competitiveness and improved innovation. Since it drives business success, businesses that embrace it will grow faster than those that don't. Besides, social media has the potential to save on time by reducing the volume of emails, reducing meeting and conference calls, saving on travel time spent to visit colleagues in other locations, reducing time spent on finding information or relevant people for a particular task. This in turn, will increase service delivery speed and improve financial performance.

Social media revenue models consists of display advertisements which follow the traditional brand exposure model, but more targeted. Branding of companies by paying application developers for exposure within their applications offer a more lucrative avenue for exposure. Virtual currency, virtual gifts and social gaming are the upcoming revenue generating models for social media.

Offering a fair chance of improving internal efficiencies while deepening relationships among employees and providing customers and stakeholders with the improved goods and services resulting from collaborative thinking, more and more organizations are embracing social media to communicate, market and sell.

F I V E

CHANGING BUSINESS DRIVERS

Social Media Platform

The world is being constantly transformed by new collaborative technologies, bringing about a participatory society and new business models. These new technologies usher in dramatic changes in business processes and even make existing ones redundant. The last decade, which can be rightly said to be a decade of social media has changed the form of communication from one-to-one to many-to-many, transforming the way in which we consume, produce and interact with information. This surge in migration to the web has signaled new approaches to marketing and customer communication and introduced a new form of business model relying heavily on social media networks. It is now an imperative for companies to harness these new platforms for marketing, interacting with customers, knowledge sharing and various other business needs. With mobile and Smartphone becoming popular and social media strengthening its grip on such mobile devices, there is an urgent need for businesses to expand their operations to these new platforms.

Social media network access has become a pre-requisite to conduct businesses. From conducting virtual business meeting to online collaborations, businesses now have power to reach out to people on the go. One of the most potent application of social media is marketing. It provides an instant dissemination of positive and negative feedback on which constant improvements can be made. Social media feedback is an innovative way of knowing customer requirements and can be used to source, improve and implement new developments. Businesses are adopting social media to recruit talent and make business connections. It is removing work-personal boundaries, organizational boundaries and Silo boundaries and making communication across a 'flatter' world faster and effective. In an economy characterized by abundance of knowledge, which must be shared, social media tools aid in faster and better information dissemination and sharing.

The next wave of social media will see more inter-connectedness through cross-postings across various social networking platforms and an intersection of social and smart mobile. While advertising is a dominant model for monetization, it will gradually decrease as the importance of social media being more than a mere advertising avenue is realized.

Social platforms and the hybrid forms of social media have the power to change the overall concept of outsourcing. There are already platforms like "Rent a Coder" where development outsourcing needs are auctioned to hundreds of companies and even individuals globally. Such platforms are futuristic from an outsourcing point of view where the customer gets choices in cost and quality from vendors across the world instead of sticking to a few vendors. Geographical and physical boundaries are no longer hurdles for any job, which can be done over the wire and hence, opens up the whole world for such services.

Facebook & LinkedIn have created a platform from casual social connecting and sharing to serious form of professional connections unheard of before. These platforms can be successfully used in creating professional online portfolios for networking and even attracting future employees, thus allowing job seekers to post their skills, abilities and resumes online and helping job recruiters find the qualified personal for their job requirement. Facebook also offers advertising access to target audience, while LinkedIn facilitates individuals and companies build and maintain professional relationships. These platform may themselves evolve over time to be useful in many more forms other than just linking, but they clearly demonstrate that such social networking tools have the potential to alter the landscape of social and professional linking of every human being.

Microblogging platforms such as Twitter, which started as a means to communicate with friends, family and coworkers, has now evolved into a powerful social medium to disseminate information quickly. Such sites help hit target audience or customers globally with a speed unthinkable a decade back.

Travel websites such as tripadvisor.com, expedia.com, travelocit.com and many other offer everything required in planning and executing a trip from locating a destination, to deals, hotels, mode of transport, restaurants and sightseeing, thus bringing the whole travel experience to an online platform. Social networking sites and mobile applications for travel are being used at every stage - right from booking flights and hotels to reading and writing hotel and restaurant reviews, posting vacation pictures on various social platforms while on vacation, using map feature and searching for attractions. Travel industry is no more constricted to travel agents and has replaced much of the commission and middlemen dependence with easy 'click' options and quick and quality service.

Online retail stores such as Amazon.com has transformed the way retail operations work today. Founded in 1994 as a new way of selling books online, today amazon.com distributes anything from books to auto parts to food items. This revolutionary model of online shopping focused on identifying consumer needs and then worked backwards to find ways to distribute the good and services they needed. Collaboration via the Internet proved an innovative response to the changing digital environment. Today more than half of the total US retail stores are web-enabled. Digital retail, a shift from the brick and mortar to the 'Click' experience, is the new means to achieve business acceleration. Shoppers have incorporated digital tools and technology into their shopping behavior, and now with the rise of Smartphones and tablets, the horizon of digital retail has further expanded. It has become imperative for brands and retailers to have successful online presence and spread to various technology platforms. Other successful online sites such as Ebay have provided even small traders a global platform to sell and buy. Thus, traditional shops have got an extension to the world at almost no additional cost.

Instant messaging platforms like Skype, Google Talk and several others have provided an alternative to email. Messaging is no more limited to typed texts but has extended to a combination of voice, data and video with no limits on sharing across any device. This has made it possible for everyone to be connected all the time.

Virtual storage and sharing platforms like Dropbox, and other cloud and file synchronization platforms have made it possible for people to access their information from any device and from any location, eliminating dependence on storage and sharing and hardware.

Pay-per-use pricing models

Pricing had not been much of an issue in the past with companies, but with clients reviewing their IT spending, focus on pricing management is much required now. New models of non-linear pricing are challenging the existing effort or time and material-based pricing model and engaging customers to pay only for what they use, sometimes even based on business results achieved. These non-linear pricing models link expenses to business, usage or productivity. In recent time, usage based pricing models or pay-per-use models have seen the highest level of adoption across industries. With the expansion of software as a service (SaaS) and the advent of cloud computing, pay-per-use pricing models are getting a further impetus. More and more customers are demanding pricing models that allow them to pay for only their usage while maintaining an even distribution of cost over time. With the software industry maturing, pay-per-use models can provide greater flexibility, eliminating the requirement of large up-front license costs and ongoing maintenance fees. This in turn will drastically bring down the cost for clients. The explosive growth in telecom in the last few decades has been attributed to user-friendly free models which allows customers to pay a 'metered fee' for only the 'service used' instead for the 'service' available. Such models are proving highly effective for small and medium businesses, that often grapple with limited cash flows.

In the early nineties, SAP platform was considered an enterprise resource planning platform only for rich companies as it required huge up-front expenses, both in cost of software and hardware and skilled labor, which were very difficult to get. Being the most successful of its kind, this package provided best practices pre-configured in the software, and companies were configured to move up the next level of efficiency in their operations. There is no doubt on the usefulness of such a platform for most of the businesses, however, not many could afford the same. Several other companies like Baan, Peoplesoft, came and established themselves in the market. Understanding the need of such packages in small sector, many other players created scaled down versions of ERP packages and some companies even created their own.

After an explosive growth of ERP over last two decades, very few players now are truly growing in that domain. SAP, the largest of such ERP players have provided SAP on cloud with a pay per use model through partners. All ERP systems now being developed are cloud-based and have effective pay per use model and a very short deployment cycle. This has spurred the growth of ERP in smaller businesses that could not have thought of affording such systems just a decade back. An example of such penetration is seen in India where thousands of small enterprises, taking advantage of good telecom, have outsourced their entire IT, depending mainly on cloud-based ERP and other services, and having just a handful of technical staff to support their team on ground.

Popularity of pay per use model will rise with time. There are plethora of applications from software development platforms to packaged applications on the cloud that have the potential to increase the usage of IT products several times through easy availability and low cost. Large companies like Microsoft are coming up with their online MS Office as a pay per use model. This will eventually lead to a fundamental change in the way businesses invested in technology and acquired technologies.

These advancements have the potential to alter the way current outsourcing takes place, causing a shift from body shopping to solutions and value based outsourcing.

Software commoditization

Commoditization takes place eventually in every successful industry as there will always be competitors who would be willing to offer the same product at a lower price or better quality. In every industry, after the initial years of settling, standards are set, bringing about greater inter-compatibility and better advancements. With a maturing industry, competing products become increasingly interchangeable commodities, allowing new industries to build atop them by creating new and innovative products, which would not have been possible had standardization not taken place. Just like the hardware companies faced competition from standardization of operating systems, which resulted in a phenomenal reduction in prices, the software industry to is being commoditized by the advent of open source free software, posing as a strong challenge to proprietary software companies.

Decades back, there was no option but to invest heavily in hardware and development of basic applications for automation of manual work. Over the years, with increase in technology needs, requirement of developers and experts increased who ended up creating similar applications in several businesses and created successful businesses around this. With increased regulations globally and standardization of product requirements in market, these processes too became almost similar. In essence, it was possible for the same application to be used, with minor changes, in several business establishments. This led to commoditization of application software. For example, SAP need not recreate the ERP for every company they install the package in. Similarly, Microsoft office is a standard globally for office productivity application. Moving down from such high level of commoditization to lower ones, examples are replete like project management, eCommerce Platforms, social interaction platforms and almost anything else. In this highly communicative centric environment with increasing standard protocols, proprietary software are becoming commodities and like any other commodity, they are being sourced by more than one producer, giving consumers the option to switch from one to another.

Software commoditization is largely driven by the rise of various communication systems such as the Internet, which depends on shared protocols. For example, a user may choose between browsers such as Internet Explorer, Mozilla Firefox or Safari, or Microsoft outlook can be replaced by Eudora or Mozilla mail or any other.

TECHNOLOGY COMMODITIZATION CURVE

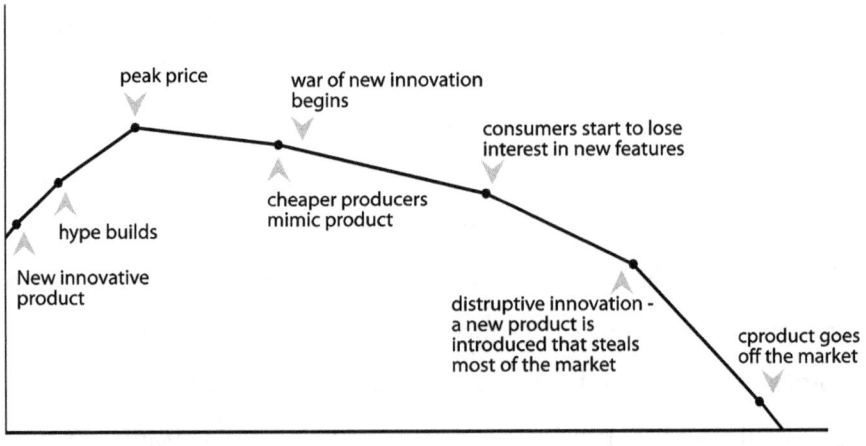

Source: simplicable.com

This is possible since they all implement the same protocols and data format. Just like any other successful industry, the software industry too is moving towards commoditization. With a maturing industry, standardization and commoditization are natural market forces. Focus on open source signals a shift in the software industry towards commoditization.

Information Technology is so widely used that few companies can claim to use it to gain a strategic advantage. To some extent, IT has made the transition to serving the same interchangeable commodities, which do not provide any specific competitive advantage over other commodities. IT vendors can no longer control their customers and command premium prices. Software entered the commoditization cycle and the spread of free and open source software has been tremendous over the last ten years, that now there is probably no software product category, particularly in the enterprise computing area, where proprietary offerings are not challenged by open source offerings.

While the commoditization has reduced the level of internal efforts companies invested in creating these things themselves, it has given rise to a different form of skills for implementation like consultants and domain experts, which are at much higher level than the ones required in body shopping. Open source platforms, end up providing the software without cost but the expert services on the software becomes the revenue model.

Changing role of CIOs

The role of a CIO, as we see today, has come a long way from a manager in Finance department responsible for accounting with a bit more technical knowledge than the rest of his accountants. The Head of Finance was the defacto chief of IT as well, until probably as recent as a decade back. This was because at that time, the scope of technology was just to automate the financial systems.

Additional job titles in the recent years from EDP Manager, MIS Manager, IT Head to CIO, are reflection to the changing role of a CIO over decades. While it has already been stated that CIO need not be a technology person but more of a business person, several progressive companies are spinning off their IT divisions to different business entities making them highly professional business organizations instead of protected entities with low level reporting. The need for such a change has evolved with IT playing a more central role from the initial support roles in any organization's success. It is almost impossible for any corporate to run without technology, not just in the form of a support role but for running their core business as well.

Changes in CIO role

Previous Role/Method		New Role/Method
Internal Provider	to	Supplier Manager
Technology Supplier	to	Technology Advisor
IT Operator	to	Business Optimizer
Back-office Focus	to	Business App Focus
Solutions Reactively	to	Strategy Proactively

Source: datacenterknowledge.com

Success of any company in market is now being measured on how capable and effective their IT systems are and how effectively they can translate the business and customer needs into revenue. Operational and strategic priority with technical management and focus on reducing cost, delivering agility and efficiency to the organization can be broadly defined as the functions of the CIO today. Technology is no more support, but it is the business. The role of a CIO therefore has evolved from support executive to a high caliber entrepreneur who has to help the business reach new heights of success.

The evolving IT and business environment characterized by rapid technological advances and increasing IT-business alignment has redefined the role of a CIO, entrusting them with more business responsibility and control than mere IT management. While the yesteryears of IT put technologist first, technical managers second and then business managers, today with IT becoming more mature, business benefits and growth is a close ally of IT practices. IT is recognized as delivering value and supporting business operations to a great extent. Thus, CIOs need both business and leadership skills along with technical capabilities to exploit the changing business models and merge them with new emerging technologies. They need to be equipped with personal leadership capabilities, technological knowledge and good business acumen.

It is very obvious that CIOs are therefore not only looking at new technologies but also looking at cost effective solutions, which can help their business flourish. They are expected to be early adaptors of new ideas and technologies. They are also key decision makers of how their technology landscape will function and how they will create the platform for their business to leapfrog to the next stage. Ineffective CIOs will be detrimental to both the success or failure of a business.

In coming times, the CIO will evolve into a thought leader and an entrepreneur, providing the guidance and execution to keep ahead of the curve and also will be responsible for the profits and losses of the organization.

Customer knowledge

Businesses today need to invest in gaining customer knowledge, treating customers as part of businesses and not outside of it. To increase access to valuable customers, evaluate the current status and profitability of a customer, companies have adopted CRM information technology, which includes leveraging technology to engage customers in a meaningful dialogue so that companies can customize products and services as per the customer's need. Adoption of CRM software packages, which include front office applications to access customers and product data and back-end systems including financials, inventory and ERP, has allowed companies to gain a competitive advantage.

Companies are able to better serve their customer through proper evaluation of customer knowledge. While CRM software packages provide customer data, this data alone does not provide any customer knowledge or insight. Specific customer information can only be generated and integrated through customer knowledge competence based on internal firm processes. This will enable firms to develop customer-specific strategies.

Customer and customer-value recognition will be very vital to the success of any business. With dozens or even hundreds of factors determining customer value and each layer providing an additional insight into consumer needs and behaviors, proper recognition by businesses will allow them to discern and anticipate specific needs and desires of their customers in order to better serve them. Technology can be appropriately harnessed to enable creating customer knowledge competencies. Using technology of social media and other interactive platforms, identification of their requirements will be easier and in turn help better translate into product or service. With the business environment now more customer-centric than product-centric, IT companies should invest in creating a knowledge-based customer recognition system to provide customer-value insight essential for businesses.

Customer Enabling technologies

While customers have been empowered and business has grown because of such changes, the old layer of middlemen has been impacted and might get replaced altogether eventually. Such changes however brings in a host of other services and possibilities which will continue to create jobs and business but will require quick change of old order to new. Those who can adapt and change would thrive in the new order. A similar impact will happen to the outsourcing model in all areas where customer need not require so many layers to get a better experience to do what is being done by them now.

Gamification

Gamification is the concept of applying game design thinking, technique and mechanisms to non–game applications and processes such as business and social impact challenges. As the number of people playing video games increases rapidly, it is rather clear that gaming is now an important part of everyday life. Hence, little surprise that it is now transiting into business environments as well. From games being used in classrooms to health care providers and surgeons using video games stimulations for practice, gaming is seeping into almost all sectors with a huge potential for engaging customers, training and encouraging desired behavior. Gamification as a business practice is becoming very popular. More and more companies are now blending games with work. Research from Gartner indicates that by the year 2015, nearly 50 percent of organizations would use gamification in various processes.

Every business is based on consumers/customers who are engaged in some behavior, be it purchasing something or subscribing to something. This behavior is what drives business value and here gamification can be used to stimulate that behavior. Gamification can be used anywhere from a media company with television shows wanting to drive contact consumption and sharing, or IT companies wanting to get people to use more of its products so that they are more likely to upgrade in the next upgrade cycle rather than move to a competitive product. Gamification transforms the workplace, which is viewed in terms of rewards and competition, providing an alternative creative and different way to solve problems by breaking the barriers and doing things differently.

Gamification makes technology more engaging and encourages users to engage in desired behaviors. It motivates people to perform tasks that are usually considered boring. Gamification can be used in employee training programmers, social networking sites, online shopping, wellness and personal activities, project management, surveys, call centers, market research and many other avenues. Inclusion of achievement badges, levels, leader boards, progress bar, virtual currency, challenges between users to embedding casual games within other activities, gamifies the process, thereby engaging and motivating the user. By accelerating feedback cycles, providing clear and well-defined goals and rules to play, building a compelling narrative, players/employees/customers can be engaged to participate and achieve the goals of the process.

Gamification primarily aims at engaging the consumer and getting them to participate, share or interact. Participation, in turn, builds a lasting relationship impacting business objectives greatly. Gamification can aid organizations to enhance brand experience by engaging users, drive active participation, encourage them to join communities, invite friends and share and ultimately turn customers into fans. It leverages both psychology and technology in ways that it can be applied outside the environment of games themselves.

CHANGE IS INEVITABLE

With the world witnessing major disruptive and transformative changes, IT needs to realign itself with these changing scenarios and focus on reducing costs, increasing the value of its operations, exploiting new opportunities and moving swiftly to seize competitive advantage. In view of the uncertainties of the economy and volatility of emerging markets, reducing cost and enhancing value should be the key focus. Companies can no longer continue to enjoy high percentage profit margins, but will need to deliver more value by doing more with less. Internal efficiency needs to increase along with proper deployment of resources for highest return, reaping more from existing investments and bolstering core competencies. Companies should be able to respond fast to implement and manage changes.

With more and more clients demanding value for the money spent, companies should focus on core capabilities along with conserving capital resources and slashing spending where there are minimal returns. Funds should be redeployed in activities that generate greater growth, more margins and provide competitive edge. But while improving time-to-value is important, companies must also work towards reaping long-term returns from investments by finding ways to get more from existing investments and improving resource efficiency.

Understanding customer requirements will enable companies to shift the customers from competitors. Flexible pricing options will further attract new customers, and retain existing ones.

Innovation will take lead and promote change and business transformation and even enable new business models. Companies need to build future capabilities by motivating existing performers, recruiting new talents and leveraging the global workforce. Innovative use of technology such as use of collaboration tools to enhance communication with customers, or leveraging technology for acquiring better and timely information will help companies mitigate many risks and enable them to act with speed in the unpredictable environment.

Greater collaboration needs to be encouraged to create a more adaptable and responsive organization. Mobile technology should be adopted for instant access to people and information and better team-based decision-making. This in turn will boost productivity of employees and reduce cost for companies, allowing them to focus on value and exploiting new opportunities. IT infrastructure should be flexible and scalable, allowing for rapid expansion and contraction. Greater standardization needs to be established, which will help increase interoperatibility and reduce cost of proprietary solutions.

S I X

CAPTIVES
(GIC)

IT holds a critical role in achieving business goals and pervades all functions and activities in the value chain. Thus the focus of outsourcing has become more than just cost saving. In recent years, GICs are becoming popular as they offer low cost service along with addition of capabilities to the parent organization. India has emerged as a favorable destination for setting up GICs due to low cost delivery, sufficient talent pool, good infrastructure and ecosystem and a growing domestic market.

Captives or GICs (Global In-house Centre) hold a significant

spot in the global service market, with India leading as the most favorable location. The GIC model was set up initially in low cost locations primarily to benefit from labor cost arbitrage. Over the years, it has continued to deliver on its promise of not just providing cost saving but adding meaningful capabilities to the parent organization. This has made the GIC model firmly established with around 4000 centers located globally. Recent years have witnessed spreading of GICs in multiple locations beyond India, and across new verticals such as manufacturing, retail, telecom, etc. GICs in India have helped India become a popular global sourcing destination offering added value to global businesses. This has led to further expansion of capacities and capabilities of Indian centers. MNCs were also prompted in exploring captive opportunities in India due to the success demonstrated by Indian IT vendors in the Y2K phenomenon. In terms of cost advantage, GICs offer saving on cost much more than third party vendors with the arbitrage sustainable for a good 12-15 years span. They aid in enhancing performance of parent organizations by providing IP protection, optimizing resource management, sourcing talents from global locations, responding quickly to changes in business environment, encouraging global best practices, harmonizing global operations, bringing about innovation and continued improvements and standardization and offering flexibility in product development. GICs further the brand of their parent organizations. Expansion to various locations globally helps organizations explore untapped markets along with accelerating time-to-market. Tailor-made processes lead to better customer satisfaction. Besides, captives aid in business continuity by effectively managing contingencies, mitigating risks and providing a disaster recovery mechanism for their parent organizations. Indian captives have greatly helped their parent organizations in consolidating operations, providing expert and efficient processes, faster time-to-market and even churned out global leadership.

It was primarily the cost arbitrage and availability of talent pool that attracted many MNCs to set up GICs in India. Though there were challenges of lack of outsourcing knowledge in the early years. However, the success of global outsourcing model demonstrated by India helped build confidence in its ability, giving a great fillip to the outsourcing industry, especially in the last decade. The growth was partially hampered due to the economic slowdown but has picked up in the past few years. Today, along with reaping cost benefits, captives are becoming innovation hubs. Organizations are driving more value from their GICs, which can serve as gateways to new expanding markets for their products and services. The last decade has seen a rapidly maturing Indian captive ecosystem. Organizations have moved from cost saving to innovation centers. Fastest sectors to mature have been ER&D/SPD (Engineering Research & Design/ Software Product Development), application development and maintenance and infrastructure management. Other sectors such as Technical and Customer Support, IT Consulting and Finance and Accounting are also rapidly maturing, followed by slow but emerging services such as Sales and Marketing, HR, Procurement and Logistics, etc.

INDIAN CAPTIVE MARKET SIZE

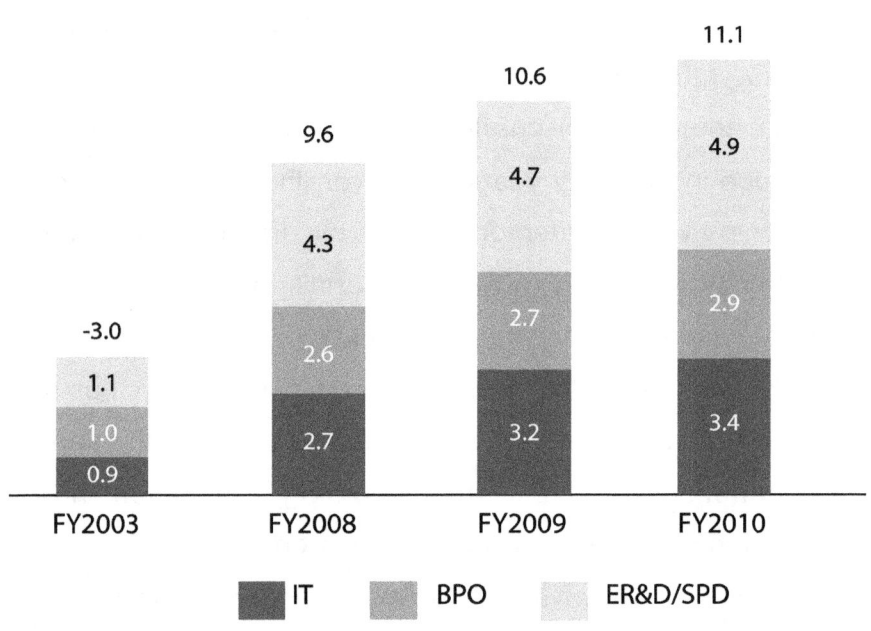

Source: NASSCOM-Zinnov analysis

While some captives in India have migrated towards enhancing value for parent organizations, other have migrated towards focusing on increasing efficiency. Out of these, most have overlapping focus on value creation by driving value for global products and opening up new markets, and enhancing economic efficiency through matured processes, stringent internal controls and measurements and a high level of automation and standardization.

The Indian GIC market has increased from USD 3 billion in FY2003 to USD 11.6 billion in FY2011, contributing 22 percent of export revenues and 1 percent of total GDP. There are about 800 GICs in India spread across IT, BPO and ER&D/SPD services. GICs are set up in various verticals such as software, telecommunications, aerospace, defense, automotive, BFSI, computer hardware, healthcare, electric, chemicals, bio-technology, etc. While maximum GICs were set up in the software semiconductors, telecommunication and banking domains between 2003-06, past years have witnessed increased investments in knowledge-based services. About 76 percent of GICs in India have their parent organization located in North America (Oracle, Dell, Hewitt, GE, HP), followed by 17 percent in Europe (HSBC, Barclays, Siemens). Of the total GICs established in India, 84 percent perform ER&D/SPD-related activities, which employees about 32 percent of the talent pool. IT outsourcing captives employ about 39 percent of the talent pool and BPO employs about 30 percent.

LOCATION OF CAPTIVES IN INDIA

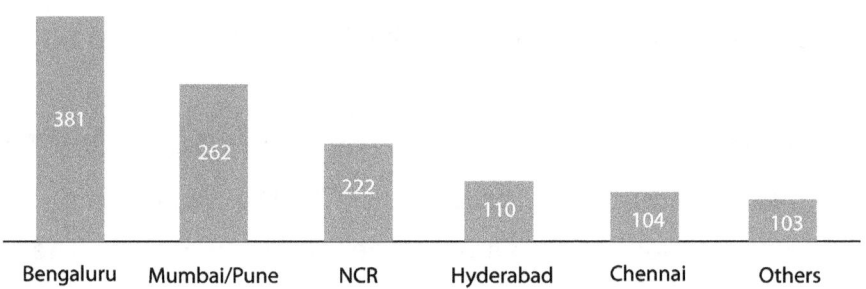

Source: NASSCOM-Zinnov analysis

Majority of captive centers in India are located in Tier 1 cities with Bengaluru being the major destination, followed by NCR, Mumbai, Pune, Chennai and Hyderabad. Tier II cities are also attracting captives for expansion and business continuity purposes. Many organizations have more than one captive located across India.

Evolution of GICs

IT outsourcing is now the top priority on every executives' agenda. The outsourcing boom, which has significantly changed industry structures, extends from single tasks to complex processes. Today the global IT outsourcing market is of a colossal size, generating billions of dollars in revenue.

Over the years, the activities being outsourced has changed from time to time. In the 1960s, computers were expensive and bulky requiring large allocation of a company's resources towards their service and maintenance. Many companies entered into contracts with service bureaus, system houses and other IT outsourcing vendors in low cost nations. Indian being the preferred destination for many, became popular for hardware related services outsourced by many nations. The advent of computer software in the 70s, created a surge in demand for software programmers. Due to insufficient labor supply in their own countries, many turned towards India for skilled labor at low cost. Thus, in the early decades, focus was primarily on cost reduction for utilization of skilled labor to bring about operational efficiency. This way, the companies could concentrate their scarce resources on core competencies and strategically outsource non-critical activities. IT activities were looked upon as non-core activities and considered not critical for the success of the business. But with increasing advancement and importance of information and communication technologies and a constantly growing dependence on IT, organizations soon realized the critical role of IT for achieving strategic goals and business success. IT emerged as a strategic business driver, delivering long-term benefits and pervading all functions and activities in the value chain. This in turn, gave IT outsourcing a new direction. The focus of IT outsourcing shifted from mere cost reduction to creating competitive advantage and fully reaping benefits of IT. Contracting for IT hardware service and maintenance and IT facilities was replaced by intellectual forms of outsourcing such as to complement for lack of internal capabilities, gain access to knowledge and exploit new possibilities for innovation. This led to strengthening of resources of the company, greater flexibility in a rapidly changing marketplace against growing global competition and uncertainties and innovation of processes, skills and technologies. From an initial phase of cost reduction venture to focusing on gaining capabilities and innovation, IT outsourcing is now in its maturity phase with focus on offering a global service model, which includes a mix of onshore, offshore and near shore outsourcing, and greater flexibility and increasing focus on product control.

DISTRIBUTION OF CAPTIVES BY HEADQUARTER LOCATIONS

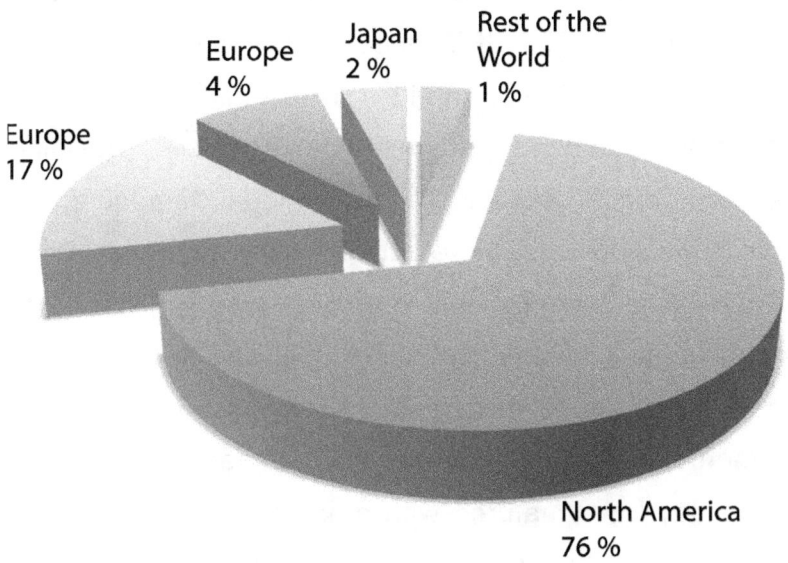

Source: NASSCOM-Zinnov analysis

MNC captives in India saw an early beginning with companies like Motorola, Texas Instruments setting up their captives in India during the early years of the Indian IT industry. Initially, they were established by organizations in search of skilled labor, who choose to set up their captive centers in India, which provided them a plethora of workforce and also a unparalleled coast arbitrage. Labor and cost arbitrage were the primary drivers for setting up captives in India. During this period, captives focused on offering basic application development services, maintenance and testing activities. BPO captives offered voice-based customer service and transactions, while ER&D/SPD centers focused on quality and product sustenance. Thus, captives in the initial years were modeled much like third party service providers, providing various back office services to their global headquarters. However, they showcased well their ability to deliver high quality service at low cost and on-time delivery. This led to MNCs cultivating captives from mere cost and talent options to transforming them into centers of innovation, product development and as a gateway into emerging markets. Captives today have matured with many serving as strategic partners with their headquarters. Focus from providing back office services has shifted to offering business analytics, product and program management, technical architecture and various functional services. Many are serving as new business units, greatly impacting the top line. BPO captives have moved up the value chain creating complete analytical models, and taking on greater leadership roles in F&A, HRO, Banking and many other sectors. They have emerged as hubs for high-end knowledge process service delivery, accounting for 50 percent of the country's knowledge-based services revenues. ER&D/SPD captives are focusing more on researching and developing new product concepts suitable for emerging markets. They have transformed into incubation centers for new innovations. Thus, captives, over the years, have evolved from being low cost back office set ups to offering knowledge-based solutions, with a more front-office approach. They have started contributing towards various design-related solutions and have proved promising in delivering break-through innovations. They are also playing a leading role in developing an R&D culture and have aided India achieve the global leader status in this sector. Captives have taken a huge initiative to spearhead a product culture, with the aim to offer affordable products to emerging markets. Success of these products will contribute significantly to overall productivity in India. A highly innovative ecosystem in the country along with nurturing skilled talent by partnering with educational institutes, search organizations and Indian companies is being promoted by the development and growth of GIC centers. New technologies have been brought to India, which were otherwise unavailable. Captive centers in India have implemented best practices in global management and processes. Moreover, they have created many entrepreneurial opportunities in the country.

MNC captives in India have witnessed an explosive growth in FY2003 recording revenue of USD 11.1 billion. They are growing at CAGR of 22 percent, contributing greatly to employment generation and GDP. Number of employees at GIC centers in India is growing at CAGR 13 percent, from a mere 150 in 2003 to 460 in 2012. Moreover, captive centers account for over 1 percent of India's GDP and support 12 million indirect employment.

Advantage of GICs

One of the most significant advantage gained from setting up GICs is the huge cost saving they continue to offer to their parent organization. GIC model of outsourcing delivers almost 45-55 percent of cost reduction for their parent companies in comparison to third party vendor outsourcing. For example, in an IT outsourcing third party arrangement, about 60-70 percent of cost is allocated towards people; 10-15 percent towards facilities; 7-10 percent towards technology; and 10-15 percent towards miscellaneous expenditures. Thus making it a total of 100 percent cost. Whereas the cost breakup for a GIC unit supporting transaction process BPO function, the setup and transition cost would amount to 2-3 percent; people cost at 13-18 percent; and another 2 percent on governance, thus making the TCO about 25-30 percent. This leaves a saving of about 45-55 percent. Thus the GIC model of outsourcing delivers a 45-55 percent of cost saving over third party vendor outsourcing.

TCO SAVINGS FOR BPO-TRANSACTION PROCESSING | US - INDIA

2012; US$ 000s per FTE per annum

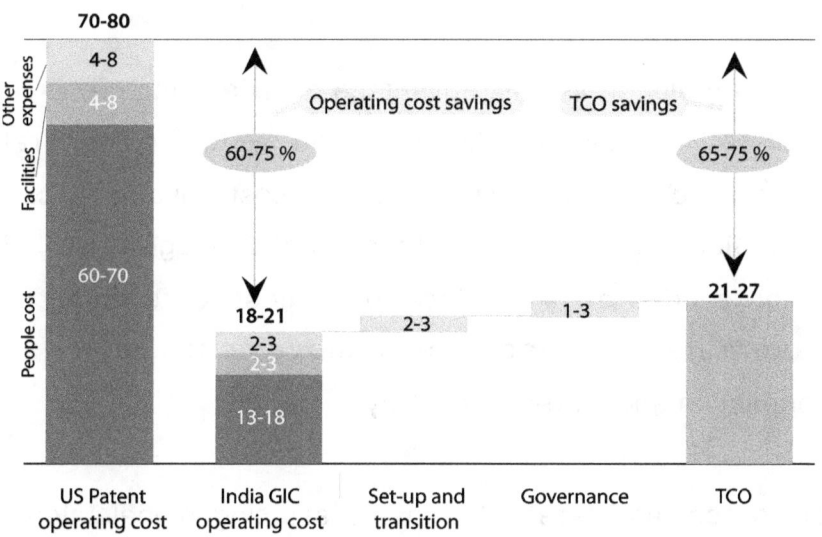

Source: Everest Group Analysis

The TCO cost varies with respect to functions to be performed by the GIC. One requiring high levels of skills would increase the people cost by some percentage. For example, there is high saving recorded for IT applications and transactions processing than complex and judgment-oriented business processes. TCO saving is also altered by locations of captives due to differences in people cost, facilities and other expenses. GICs further hold a promising scenario of sustaining this cost arbitrage for the next 12-15 years with minor ups and downs owing to inflation of wages and rising cost of other facilities and fluctuations in currency.

GICs can prolong this cost advantage by increasing resource utilization, improving efficiency and reducing general administrative expenses. However, this cost advantage can be disrupted due to exceptional factors of shortage of skilled workforce, decrease in location's cost difference or unfavorable macroeconomic movements such as hyperinflation and currency volatility.

Besides cost arbitrage, GIC enable sourcing global talents thus helping organizations build high levels of skills and capabilities. IP is retained within the company and its various wholly-owned subsidiaries. This helps organizations maintain their competitive edge in the market. GICs provide organizations more flexibility to adjust to changing business situations along with a better control over its operations across various locations. GICs set up in various locations open the door to new markets and also opens up new avenues for generating more revenue streams through production of customized products or services in the new markets. Moreover, GICs encourage innovation and R&D. The knowledge and ideas of the organization are retained within the captives, which operate like subsidiaries of the parent organizations and are thus constantly improved upon. Third party vendors on the other hand, do not guarantee protection of IP, nor offer the possibility of opening up new markets for the clients. Besides, there is significantly less focus on innovation and talent development, whereas the cost is higher than captives. Thus GIC scores high on all parameters as compared to third party vendors.

IT captives (Global In-House Centers)

IT captives are well established across various verticals ranging from BFSI, retail, software, semiconductors, electronics and telecommunication. One of the key reason for organizations to choose India as a suitable destination for IT captives is the availability of IT services talent, which is generated by the rapid growth and development of service providers in India. The software captives are the most popular amounting to 28.5 percent of total IT captives in India, followed by BFSI contributing about 17 percent IT captives. IT captives have increased in number over the years from 45 before 2000 to more than 150 captives at present, thus representing an increase of almost 240 percent in the past 10 years, along with rapidly rising revenue from USD 0.9 billion to more than USD 7 billion.

Within IT captives, about 75 percent of total talent pool is allocated towards BFSI, which has the maximum representation across 23 global banks with captives in India, followed by software, which is the second largest in headcount. The telecom vertical is also fast emerging with more than 15 organizations operating captives for activities ranging from application development, system integration to IT consulting. The average headcount for IT captives in India is about 650.

Maximum IT captives are set up by organizations from North America, followed by Europe. North America captives also generate the maximum revenue. In terms of locations of IT captives, most are concentrated in Bengaluru followed by Mumbai, Pune, NCR, Hyderabad and Chennai. Bengaluru continues to host the maximum number of IT captives. The main function performed by IT captives in India is testing services and maintaining internally build IT applications for the day-to-day operations of the organization. This is followed by application development, the second most popular function performed by IT captives. Application development provides for developing customized applications for the organization's internal usage. The next popular function includes infrastructure management service like database administration, web operations, desktop management, service desk, incident management, etc. Other functions such as system and network integration are also becoming popular as captives are maturing in their operations. IT consulting is another niche area, which is fast becoming popular with many captives ahead on the maturity curve. Application development and maintenance activities are primarily driven by the BFSI vertical, but are also spreading into new verticals such as retail. Increasing adoption and utilization of new technologies such as cloud, SOA has led to inflow of high value work. Consulting services are also gaining momentum with decreasing license revenues for product organizations. Captives are now offering a leading role in consulting-led services from earlier playing a mere support role. Infrastructure management services offshoring is also nudging ahead with services being evolved from simple help desk support to more complex architectural design and network planning, requiring experienced professionals.

Testing services, which are an important part of offshoring business for many captives, are adopting new cloud based technologies for automating processes. They are coming up with innovative business models to enable greater flexibility and standardization of testing processes. This mature way of testing is a good replacement for traditional models of testing, requiring allocation of dedicated resources and creating of entire plan for testing processes. Testing is now using the cloud approach to access cases or pre-build scenarios. Cloud offers a great value proposition with easy searching facility and customization and a powerful analytical engine. This has drastically reduced the time and effort spent in testing and is a cheaper option in the long run.

BPO Captives

Realizing the increasing advantage of BPO captives, organizations are setting up captives for carrying out research, consulting and knowledge-based services. The BPO captive market accounts for 26 percent of the total captive market with the number of captives steadily on the rise from 26 in FY2000 to 111 in FY2009. Well represented in all verticals such as software, research, consulting, BFSI, telecommunication, etc, BPO captives in India have been generating increasing revenues every year. BFSI vertical has the maximum number of captives performing various voice and non-voice functions for global customers. Software is the second most popular vertical for BPO activities, followed by research and consulting, computer hardware, telecommunication and healthcare. The BPO captive sector is largely dominated by large organizations setting up captives as most small organizations prefer third party providers for outsourcing BPO related activities due to cost limitations. Most of these big organizations are based in US. Financial capital Mumbai has the largest number of BPO captives, followed by Bengaluru, NCR, Chennai and Hyderabad.

Various BPO services are offered in India such as Finance and accounting, customer interaction services, knowledge based services, sales and marketing, HR, procurement and logistics. Of these finance and accounting forms the major focus with almost 27 percent captives offering this service. Customer interaction and support services accounts for about 20 percent of BPO captive revenue, along with a great amount delivered from performing high level L3,L4 and L5 support for hi-tech companies across the globe. Finance and accounting is the most popular function offered by BPO captives in India, largely dominated by the BFSI, utilities and healthcare verticals, and with constantly evolving talent pool, offshoring in finance and accounting is bound to grow further in the future. Finance and accounting captives in India are gradually evolving into finance and accounting shared services centers, providing high value and enhanced savings to their headquarters. HR outsourcing involving workforce administration, leave management, payroll, recruitment and staffing is at a relatively nascent stage but is showing signs of rapid maturity with now even small organizations outsourcing HR activities to India. Within inside sales value services, planning and identification, lead generation, requirement analysis and fulfillment are typically outsourced to India, which provides a fairly large talent pool, time zone advantage, good regional market understanding and penetration to APAC markets. India centers often host online demonstrations for potential customer, helping them with product information.

Knowledge-based services are increasingly being outsourced to captives in India, which could soon become a knowledge based services hub. Knowledge based services provide business intelligence by collecting data from organizations for making strategic decisions. Many organizations have dedicated knowledge teams for HR and finance and accounting activities to provide data such as projected attrition, requirements for new candidates, etc, thus helping organizations in faster decision making.

ER&D/SPD Captives

Availability of high talent pool for ER&D/SPD segment in India is one of the chief driver for the fastest growth of this segment within the captive industry in India. The ER&D/SPD sector has been witnessing an exponential growth since 2003, with revenues reaching USD 4.9 billion in FY2010, and a CAGR of 24 percent over the last few years. Offshoring of engineering service design activities has picked up in the last decade and off late many automotive and aerospace organizations are setting up ER&D captive in India. ER&D/SPD captives are found in verticals such as software, telecommunications, semiconductors, industrial, automotive, aerospace, defense, etc, with more than 22 captives generating more than 10 billion revenue. The ER&D/SPD segment employs over 110 thousand employees, with small R&D centers representing a significant portion of global R&D headcount. Due to greater sharing of product ownership and responsibility, these R&D captives are also serving as significant innovation hubs.

Maximum ER&D/SPD captives have their parent organizations in North America, which contributes to almost 70 percent of the total captive market. Bengaluru hosts the maximum number of ER&D/SPD captives, followed by Mumbai, Pune, NCR, Hyderabad and Chennai.

Embedded systems, engineering services and software product development are the major focus areas for ER&D/SPD captives in India. With increasing maturity in service delivery, more and more captives are undertaking architectural design activities. Moreover, with new emerging markets, organizations are commanding more product ownership from Indian centers for creation for localized products and services and in the process driving up innovation and value creation of parent organizations. In fact innovation and access to new markets are the new drivers for captives in India, replacing the earlier drivers of cost arbitrage and talent pool, mainly due to slowing of growth in developed markets and increasing focus on emerging markets. Thus ER&D captives are now focusing on increasing maturity of their captives to help create greater competency for their parent organizations.

Organizations are looking beyond cost benefit and availability of talent pool to focus on developing products for local markets, innovation, increasing productivity and ownership, capability development and business model innovation and leveraging a start up ecosystem. Captives in India are encouraging this shift towards new focus areas by creating location-specific competencies, developing domain expertise in certain areas, encouraging proper project selection, improving organization alignment to enable joint decisions among business heads and global unit heads, driving innovation for local market, increasing knowledge levels and inculcating a highly customer-led innovation culture.

India as the preferred destination

From starting as a low cost location serving routine technology services for global organizations, India has, over the years, matured in its outsourcing offerings and capabilities to providing integrated services, large scale contracts, product and services design capabilities, knowledge management, legal processes and many others. Today, practically any outsourcing service can be performed in India, offering utmost benefit of cost, quality and innovation. With the emergence of domestic market in India, many organizations have set up captives in India focusing on developing services and products for new markets. There are various factors responsible for making India as a favorable option for global sourcing:

1. Low cost delivery

India is the most financially attractive location for outsourced services as compared to Asian, European and South American countries. Outsourcing to Tier 1 Indian cities works out very reasonable in terms of cost and the recent shift towards outsourcing to Tier 2 cities is offering a 20-30 percent further reduction in operating cost. Most leading global companies such as IBM, CISCO, Oracle, etc, have set up outsourcing or captive bases in India. India has a plethora of skilled workforce, with labor cost much lower than many Asian countries. Moreover, wage inflation in India is not very high. With 75-80 percent delivery workforce comprising of junior entry-level programmers accounting for 10-15 percent individual wage hike, and 20-25 percent workforce comprising of senior level programmers and managers accounting for 4-8 percent individual wage hike, the average wage inflation remains at 11-12 percent. And this can be reduced to 6-8 percent per annum by proactively managing talent with entry-level resources.

2. High capability talent pool

India has the world's largest pool of employable talent. Professional expertise is available at a cost most developed countries cannot offer. The number of graduates in India is steadily increasing offering high caliber expert skills. Indian education system can boast of being the second largest pool of engineers and scientist in the world with around 5200 engineering colleges and more than 1500 research institutes. This robust education system produces more than 750000 post graduates every year who are well versed in English language and thus removing all language and speech barriers.

3. Robust infrastructure ecosystem

The quality of infrastructure in India in comparable to other developed locations. The government and private organizations have made tremendous efforts and developments to build an infrastructure conducive to attracting global companies for outsourcing opportunities.

Setting up of software technology parks and offering SEZ schemes has played a crucial role in the advancement of the industry. Indian telecom ranks amongst the largest and fastest growing market in the world with rapidly increasing subscriptions every month. The telecom revolution has slashed the average call rate by 70 percent and handset prices by 50 percent, allowing ready connectivity and world class service at low cost. The government and private sector has increased the number of educational institutions churning out engineering and other expert talents. A focused approach to cultivate a skilled workforce, which is well versed in technology and spoken English has been one of the main attraction for companies looking to outsource. Besides, various tax incentives and policies favoring the development of IT has helped India become a viable location, providing ease of operation, without interference.

4. Growing Indian Market

India has become the fourth largest economy in the world in terms of Purchasing Power Parity, resulting in an increase in spending capacity of citizens, doubling of average household income and emergence of new middle class. A continuation on this high growth path would lead to a transformation of the social pyramid with more households moving upwards from poverty and the middle class swelling by a great percentage. Thus a rapidly growing economy and rising middle class presents a huge market in India itself. Many companies are taking advantage of this new developed market for their products and services as well as channelizing to other developing nations by setting up shops in India.

5. Innovation-conducive environment

Units set up in India are evolving an innovation conductive environment by focusing on developing new technologies, streamlining and augmenting business processes, innovating internal processes, encouraging employees to innovate, experimenting with new business models and focusing on IP creation. Many large organizations have set up in-house research labs for carrying out extensive R&D. Many companies are aligning with educational institutions to help bring the talent abreast with changing business environment. There has been a shift in the focus from process innovation done in the past to core technology innovations, which in terms brings about innovations to internal processes. IP creation has got a new boast along with new technology development, model and process innovation.

MATURING CAPTIVE LANDSCAPE

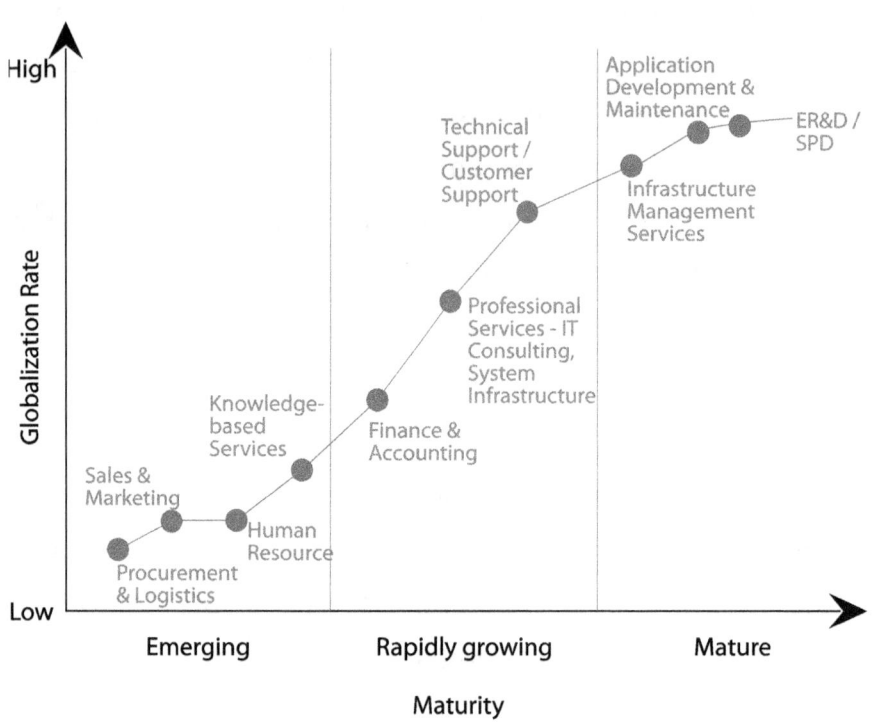

Source: NASSCOM-Zinnov analysis

6. Global footprint

India has showcased to the world its technological capabilities and skills, which is unmatched when compared with many developing nations. The growth of the IT industry in India has been phenomenal. India has continually expanded its horizons, entered new markets, continued to offer a wide range of services along with constantly moving up the value chain. Today, Indian players perform high value complex business-critical services. This established footprint over the years has build confidence of many organizations which are aiming at reaping more value based advantages from their Indian units.

Challenges before GICs

Despite the tremendous success showcased by captives, they are behest with a number of challenges in terms of rising cost, talent crunch, lack of sufficient innovation, low levels of productivity and problems of business continuity.

Escalating cost is one of the chief concerns of organizations with captive centers in India. Captives follow global standards in their operations, technology and infrastructure, which can add to the overall cost of operation. This rising cost, which has been increasing over the past few years, is a major deterrent to India's competitiveness. In terms of cost inflation, best in class captives have recorded lesser operating cost than median captives, which have almost double the level of operating cost. This gap between the best in class captives and median captives can be largely attributed to differences in business practices followed. Focus on effectively managing talent by hiring the right skilled people, setting adequate job expectations and building a visible career path will result in lower attrition even at lower compensation levels, thus providing an almost 35 percent operation cost advantage. This needs to go hand in hand with increasing productivity by multi-skilling workforce to minimize idle time. This can help achieve 20 percent cost advantage. And a robust infrastructure can add an additional 25 percent cost advantage.

High attrition rates is another concern for captives in India, especially since captives do not maintain a bench nor hire extensively from campuses. However, even in terms of rate of attrition, best in class captives have significantly lower attrition rate as compared to median captives. Best in class captives also pay lower wages, thus eliminating the compensation factor for driving attrition. Successfully cross-skilling people, developing a career path for them, grooming them for leadership positions, focusing on retaining team and encouraging employees to build long term relations have been some of the key reasons for best in class captives maintaining a low attrition rate.

An inadequately experienced and skilled talent pool is another challenging issue faced by captives in India. To address this problem, many innovative strategies have been adopted by best in class captives to develop talent through various expat programs, cross-center mentorships programs, internal training programs and partnering with universities for research projects. Many are allocating greater ownership to employees for managing end-to-end tasks along with consistently mentoring them for the next leadership level. Captives are also focusing on increasing innovation to drive greater opportunities. They are constantly tapping into new markets in developing countries and value segments in wealthy countries, thus shifting focus from developed to emerging markets. Building of local teams is being encouraged, offering them greater autonomy to develop their strategies and products and focus on problems of customers in emerging markets. Moreover, disruptive technologies are being adopted, with products taking root in simple applications at the bottom of the market but with a potential to move upmarket and even disrupting established competitors. All these measures will help develop simple products for emerging segments and markets, give access to new customer and bring about global scalability. Innovation is now the dominant theme for captive expansion. More and more captives are enabling innovation by setting up innovation labs, collaborating tools, reforming and revamping organizational structures and holding numerous workshops and seminars to increase knowledge base.

Another challenge for captives in India has been low productivity as cited by their parent organizations. According to them, individual productivity at the Indian centers is much lower than that at the headquarters. However, again best in class captives have managed better productivity through proper development of talent, optimizing processes, building adequate labs, infrastructure for innovation, bringing about automation of models and processes, eliminating wastage, forecasting accurate volumes, cross-skilling workforce and initiating strong training programs. Setting up of captives in Tier 2 cities, which offer low cost options, is emerging as a good alternative to Tier 1 cities, which are now experiencing rising costs. Many MNCs have set up captives in Tier 2 cities like Coimbatore, Mysore, Madurai, etc. The state governments in Tier 2 cities have also encouraged this development and have made efforts to promote their cities as R&D and IT service hubs. They have set up software technology parks and offered various tax incentives to bring about IT development.

GICs are reaching a stage of maturity where they can transform core business models of their parent organizations, drive growth and innovation to gain a competitive advantage, increase client segments, build presence in new locations and significantly boost revenues. GICs have a structural advantage over third party providers as they enjoy access to offshoring advantage along with greater integration with the parent organization. This allows them to deliver more complex products, have a better learning curve, greater knowledge development due to IP protection and access to superior talent. GICs are maturing to fully benefit from this cost and talent offshoring proposition and the additional benefit of in-house business model. GICs are focusing on creating additional opportunities of expertise in domains, scaling up in operations and encouraging mature leadership. This has led to strengthening of parent companies confidence in GIC, enabling the GICs to move up value creation. Through improving productivity and customer experience, applying best practices across organizations, expanding research and analytics capabilities, expanding service or process scope, entering new markets and developing products for new markets, GICs can greatly become revenue centers, adding more value than mere labor cost arbitrage. And value addition is soon becoming an imperative for GICs to retain their relevance. It will enable GICs to transform the core business of their parent organization and help address the many challenges they presently face. In order to sustain value creation, GICs need changes in organizational approaches in terms of operating models, especially as the focus of parent organizations starts shifting from cost benefit and execution to generating more value for them. To drive this value, GICs need global functional integration and a strong local leadership support. There should be constant engagement between CEOs and business stakeholders across locations so that the changing opportunities offered by GICs can be incorporated in strategic business decisions. Collaboration between local and offshore centers should be encouraged to facilitate client proximity required for innovation. GICs should constantly move away from getting into 'comfort zones' by pushing their benchmarks and striving for greater value creation.

FUTURE MODELS OF VALUE IN OUTSOURCING

India has positioned itself as a major destination for outsourcing, but with the dynamics of global businesses changing; outsourcing will also undergo a change. New forms of outsourcing will replace the existing ones and outsourcing will spread to several areas, which are either already being done in a nascent form or will re-emerge in another form. India has so far been able to evolve with changing needs. IT still stands out for offering low cost efficient service. Today as customers look beyond cost effective solutions and towards enhanced productivity, exceptional quality and business process excellence, India with its multi-skilled people promises a bright future for outsourcing.

Holistic BPOs and KPOs

Challenging economic factors have forced organizations to evaluate their use of BPO initiatives. Increasing competition, over the years, in retail, CPG and telecommunications has further led to evaluation of the use of BPO. With BPO moving away from transaction processing towards driving business value, clients too have expectations beyond cost advantage and are seeking outsourcing as an aid to better business operations, with more industry-specific offerings and outsourcing mid and front office services. Thus the future of BPO and KPO projects a more holistic outlook, with end-to-end service delivery and clear outcome in terms of business.

Currently, most of the BPO work is in form of outsourcing a particular processing to India, such as bill settlement, bank reconciliation or employee background check. While hundreds of processes are being performed, very few companies have end-to-end business accountability. In the coming times, this will change in the form of taking over end-to-end processing, right from purchase orders to payment processing and even arranging for goods receipt confirmation to the customer's work place. Costing of such services would be at a fixed cost per transaction or pay-per-use model, instead of one time contract fee. Such an offering will provide the customer greater convenience in terms of saving unwanted cost, lesser re-work between departments, better data management and assure them an outcome in the desired form, thereby leading to enhanced business performance.

While pricing benchmarks have been established by BPO service providers, their key selling point will be of providing service benchmarks, with metrics for transaction turnaround time, accuracy and other duality measures. Along with setting service benchmarks, BPO need to focus on building mature business models and improving methodologies. Buyers will look beyond mere cost saving to reaping additional benefits of transformation and innovation. KPOs too will need to be equipped with exceptional business, financial and analytical insight and enhance ability to tackle supply chain challenges. Given the huge volume of transactional data, the ability to accurately analyse it, understand and derive insights and identify opportunities for value addition too the customer's business is what the future BPO and KPO service providers will be aiming at. Moreover, outsourcing will be taken as a partnership with the service provider, who will take on a more consultant-like role and take part in the decision-making process as well as share the risk.

Pay per use for every technology services

Over the past few years, outsourcing pricing models and contract vehicles have evolved quiet a lot. Pressures on companies to reduce cost of operation and protect capital will continue to remain. Along with cost benefit, buyers are now also seeking continuous improvements. While short-term cost saving and labour arbitrage satisfies the immediate needs, an approach towards innovation to deliver additional value will be the focus moving ahead.   There are hardly any price differentiations left in delivering outsourcing services leaving the service provider with no pricing powers. Advancements in technology has made predicting the price for 12 months out difficult, giving further impetus to a flexible usage based pricing model that can constantly adapt to the changing market conditions. Thus in the coming years, focus will shift to pay per use models with service providers becoming strategic partners. They will need to rapidly mature from the traditional effort-based pricing model to transaction-based pricing and eventually to outcome-based model, which will create a direct relationship between cost and business result.

Pay per use model will cover almost all the technology services and will blur the boundary between outsourcing and buying of readymade services. From basic infrastructure like data centre (Cloud) to network, hardware, software and even custom packages will also become targets for pay per use model. Benchmarking standard pricing will also enable greater transparency. Organizations will demand more price variability along with option for easy low cost exit from long-term contracts. Service providers will no longer be looked upon as cost centers, but as value centers. Pay per use pricing model also helps the service provider capitalize on economies of scale as by setting up the infrastructure that is charged on a pay per use basis to multiple clients, the service provider is able to absorb the individual peaks and troughs of demand. Thus, this model is economically efficient and maximizes value for both parties.

CIO to run IT as a business

Advancements in technology, advent of social media, business intelligence, big data, cloud and mobility have brought about a paradigm shift in the way IT is viewed today from automating operations to aligning IT with business for strategic advantage. These significant technological changes, growing impact of social platforms, enterprise collaboration strategies and rapid IT consumerization has led to a need to devise new and innovative operational and investment models. Against this background, the role of the CIO is also evolving, as he needs to focus on developing technology-led innovation and essentially operate every technology services as a business for their enterprise.

The CIO will play a central role in operations and strategic decision-making to enable innovation for the business and thereby decrease the growing disconnect between user expectation and the services being delivered. The pressure to deliver more with less will continue and the CIO will be expected to bring about profitable growth along with business agility. While most of the services will be outsourced or bought on pay per use model, CIOs will have a duty to make maximum use of the data and technology resources available to the organization in minimum time and at optimal cost. CIO's role will evolve from technocrat to a business leader who will help organization realize maximum benefits out of the data and information the organization has to convert into customers and revenue. The CIO will play a pivotal role in operational and commercial strategy. Focus on business will be important and the CIO will be expected to have a business background with an interest in technology rather than the other way around. Funds used by companies to merely 'keeping the IT lights on' will be diverted to fund IT initiative that will add on to business productivity.

Talent creating Industry

With more and more companies focusing on innovating processes and business strategies and working on technology-led innovations, a skill set conducive to bringing about such transformations will be required. Creating and nurturing talent will be a big industry beyond just schools and colleges.

Talented person of tomorrow will not be someone who has a degree from college and has proven once on the job, but someone who continuously keeps getting educated with a motive of continuously being relevant to the business needs.

Talent will be in high demand by companies who would look at innovating processes and available technologies to give better reach to customers. Level of education would be of very high quality and more than just obtaining a degree or completing a certification. It would focus on nurturing creativity and innovative thinking. User organizations will always look for key technology talents who would help the organization innovate with new ideas to reach customers and increase revenue. Those who would actually carry out the execution of such ideas would only need commodity skills, which would take a back seat while skills of innovative thinking and business strategizing would be in high demand. Commodity skills would be mostly taken care of by body shopping companies. IT talent would be developed in line with business strategies and not just commodity skills. It will not be uncommon to see formal education loosing out to business relevant knowledge and online education become one of the major source of knowledge.

Captives (Global In-house Centers)

Enterprises are focusing more on innovation, making presence in new geographies, expanding customer base, spreading to new markets and boosting revenue through newer business models. They are looking beyond cost arbitrage and delivery efficiency. On the other side, third party vendors offering traditional outsourcing have only labour and cost arbitrage to offer. But with both cost of operation and labour rising, increasing competition, and companies now looking for more than just cost and labour advantage, third party vendors are finding it challenging to attract and retain customers. Captives or wholly owned subsidiaries provide lower cost than the price charged by third party vendors along with better control, security and flexibility. Sharing of assets, intellectual property and core business activity between the parent organization and its subsidiary leads to better operational excellence and better customer satisfaction. Thus captives offer the offshoring advantages of cost and talent and also additional benefits of value generation due to their integrated model. This will in turn impact the business of existing IT outsourcing companies and would push them further down the value chain. The future will see captives having majority share of high end technology work, relegating IT companies to act as fillers to uneven demands and niche talents for short periods of time. This will also impact the Indian IT companies in terms of revenues and growth in their traditional body shopping business.

Need for lower cost will always remain and will get supplemented but not replaced with anything else.

Drastic cost cutting measures adopted by companies and increasing competition among service providers has drastically brought down the prices. In times to come, offering low cost will be a given fact and no more the reason to pitch for business. The key to future business will be innovation, value generation, quality and ownership, which can help company stand out and attract and retain more customers. Thus from offering low cost solutions, the main thrust will be to be able generate value for the clients. Clients will also shift their focus from cost cutting to improving processes and innovating. Though resource constraints may remain and companies will look at doing more with less, but they will be more focused on value addition, which means they will now aim at doing more with less but doing it better. Short-term cost gains would be replaced by long term strategies aiming to simplify business processes and develop and deploy systems and applications more effectively. Reasons for converting business will be more if it can lead to significant changes without impacting business than merely shifting to a new technology.

Body shopping as done today will reduce

Body shopping lifecycle for technology services has reached its peak and will reduce significantly from the level it is today. Over the years, body shopping has been offering twin benefits of labour cost arbitrage and economies of scale, but customer are now looking beyond these benefits and seeking technology enablers for best business processes in a cost-effective manner. Commodity resources being aplenty, the cost of body shopping will further slash making it challenging for vendors to maintain a continuous inventory of technologically trained manpower. While body shopping takes care of managing the process and people, the technology is managed by customer and thus leads to no value addition to the client's business. Customers in the future would expect more technology-led process transformations, and there will be high demand for technologies which would be enablers to business rather than just technological advancements. The future of outsourcing would entail an innovative service delivery model where end-to-end processes would be offered. Technological services would be standardized and consolidated into solutions and product portfolios and they will be based on pay per use pricing models. Outsourcing would imply end-to-end processes from implementing and managing outsourced process, people and technology to aligning them with the business objectives of the customers. Those who will provide end-to-end solution will be more preferred over those service providers who merely provide labor. Companies just providing consulting and not taking ownership of implementing the recommendations will not be preferred over someone who can do that. This synergic coming together of traditional outsourcing with technology-led transformations will lead to value creation, additional cost saving, process optimization, economies of scale and innovation. Body shopping would have a holistic view of people process and technology.

Outcome based contracts

As businesses will start expecting more value from IT vendors, there will clear metrics of "value", which will govern outsourcing contracts in the future. Financial constraints and budgetary pressures will force businesses to work in tandem with vendors and provide them access to their business so as to make them strategic partners in achieving the business objectives. Vendors too, would need to focus more on understanding the client's business as a whole and not restrict themselves to IT alone. The overall outsourcing relationship between the client and the vendor is a complex one, because while the two retain their individual identities and competitiveness, they need to function together towards a common goal. More and more business in the future will opt for service agreements and key performance indicators that promise delivery of value rather than attempt to simply reduce the cost. Expectations of clients would be cleared out at the onset of the engagement and drafted into the deliverables, with defined metrics of value. Vendors would move beyond cost and process efficiency and move towards outcome based contracts, which mean to be paid on performance rather than based on the number of people deployed. This will result in elimination of waste from processes, optimal utilization of resources and people and natural betterment of services. With the client and vendor becoming inter-dependent, risk will be shared between the two, which the vendor can cover by including a risk premium in the price. Outsourcing engagements will start becoming more and more standard.

Multi-sourcing

Earlier organizations outsourced entire IT responsibility to vendors, but in the future the trend will shift towards best of breed outsourcing selections and multi-sourcing. Large deals will either be multi sourced at customer's end or will have extensive multi sourcing done by the service providers. Multi sourcing would provide the client with the option of an immediate available backup in case the primary supplier fails to meet the quality standards. The customer would retain the freedom to allocate services or projects between various service providers thus achieving best results from all outsourced contracts. The customer will also be able to define and change the scope of service and thereby encourage competition to reduce cost, improve quality and attentiveness. Multi sourcing concept will impact large IT players as it will help smaller players to pitch with best services to their clients. It will ultimately result in greater cost savings and better efficiency as the client moves from managing one supplier in a scope of serve to managing a competitive supply chain. It will also help in risk management as few customers will be willing to put their entire risk in a single basket unless they are not significant in size themselves. Managing multi sourcing however would need dedicated efforts from the customer for better coordination and program management to get better results.

Greater transparency

As the number of IT companies goes on increasing, customers have a plethora of choice when it comes to allocating their resources and revenues in contracts that reap them maximum benefits. The IT companies in the future will have more transparency than before and business will be driven through reviews and ratings, much like the review and rating system of Trip-advisor, which reviews hotels as given by the users. Trip Advisor type of rating and review agencies will in the future rate IT companies, projects and even IT managers and their abilities. Greater transparency in the workings of IT companies will reduce opportunity for misuse of resources, build better confidence of the client in the vendor's ability and act as a motivational tool for them to deliver exceptional results. Companies will take their image more seriously and will work harder to retain the customers. However, focus on retaining customers will be beyond the sales pitch and will be through offering better products, services and greater value. Image making will become important for companies as a favorable brand image will help them gain a competitive advantage over their competitors. Companies will have to make efforts to retain the brand image as it takes a lot of time to build a good image but only one negative report may undo years of good work.

India as a global R&D hub

With the global R&D offshoring business to India reaching US $13.10 billion in 2011, R&D holds the promise of becoming a large outsourcing industry in India. With availability of talented workers and cost and geographical location advantage, India scored over many other nations as a choice for R&D outsourcing. Along with these factors, emergence of various macro themes like emerging markets, cloud computing, enterprise adoption and convergence and mobility are driving growth in R&D. While early efforts by multinational companies to set up R&D in India were mainly due to the need to 'localize' products, now much encouraged by the success of Indian BPO, multinationals are looking at research process outsourcing. Companies are expecting the fastest growth in the future to come from Asian countries mainly India and China. To propel this growth of R&D, India needs to establish a good intellectual property protection system to enable high level of trust in making these companies contribute. Also in the future, India will provide a large market in itself and R&D efforts will be directed to tap the growing Indian market and their specific needs. Global companies would test out their products in India before rolling out elsewhere to ensure low failure.

Cloud computing everywhere

Business in the future will need to embrace a connected ecosystem approach to remain afloat. Cloud will be the preferred mode of service delivery with more and more generic software and platforms being made available on the cloud. Companies will migrate to cloud as the most viable solution for mission critical business applications. Cloud will eliminate large parts of in-house IT structures, offering a better economic model, low cost, greater efficiency and new capabilities. Scalability and business agility would be very important factors for companies, given the transforming business environment and hence adoption of cloud will be encouraged as cloud satisfies both these factors. People will have access to software applications online through a network server and not be dependent on tools and information housed on their personal computers. Cloud computing would expand exponentially and come to dominate all information transactions. It would also drive more consumption of IT services at a very affordable cost.

New models of software development

Software development will no more be confined to closed offices in couple of locations but will be available as a service from any location and any time. As SaaS adoption increases, traditional software application vendors could face fierce competition and extinction. Virtual software development will be popularized and talent will not be required to relocate. Virtual teams would collaborate and execute a project from multiple locations, thus allowing organizations to get projects done quickly and utilize skills of workers even if they are geographically dispersed. This will also allow service providers to hunt for talent everywhere and contribute a wide range of expertise and knowledge to a particular task, thus also resulting in challenging poor and substandard services.

Platform development will continue to drive the upper technology levels and more and more such platforms will be contributed to open source. This will in turn create communities and drive developments, which will keep taking technology to new heights. Android and iOS platforms today are platforms of choice for low cost and affordable development for developers who use these platforms to enrich the experience of iOS and Android devices. Many more such platforms will continue to be developed. Outsourcers will find a lot more coming to them in form of such practices like what we see today as iOS and Android practices which rake in millions by vendors who are quick to encash such opportunities. However, these opportunities will continue to come and go and vendors will have to continue to invest in up skilling their employees all the time.

Vendors as strategic partners

In a path-breaking trend, progressive companies will involve their key vendors to become part of their decision-making and boardroom decisions. Strengthening relations between customer and their vendors as they become strategic partners will help in collectively achieving the goal of the company. As IT aligns more with business, vendors would need to be made part of more and more decision-making processes of their customer's business. The strategic implications of emerging technology will continue to increase and managers would need to choose technology vendors that are not just suppliers but strategic business partners.

Indian IT Industry will overhaul

Indian IT has been witnessing tenfold rise since the Y2K glitch pushed the industry onto the world stage. But now the industry is facing challenges of rising cost in cities and wage inflation. At the same time, European economies are becoming more protective about retaining jobs due to continuous job pressures and are thus discouraging outsourcing to India. India is also facing tough competition from low wage countries like Philippines, Eastern Europe and Latin America. Complex and expensive software deployments are giving way to cheaper and less complex models. Thus, the current model of outsourcing will continue to become less attractive as margins reduce and logistics become more complex.

All these challenges are likely to impact Indian IT outsourcing even more in mid and long term. In order to retain its dominant position, India would have to move up the value chain in service delivery to justify the premium. Moving from service to developing products will also allow companies to grow revenues. Tier 2 and 3 cities would need to be developed to utilize untapped resources. Focus will have to be shifted towards doing more intellectual work than just labor work. Companies will need to invest substantially to keep a positive media image so as not to create any negative sentiments regarding outsourcing but project it as a better opportunity.

Rising internal consumption in India

Internal consumption in India will rise manifold making it very attractive to invest within the country. Indian consumption of IT will also increase in same ratio. India will face US like situation with outside companies bidding and challenging Indian companies in the local market itself. The market however, will be very different to what most of the companies have so far worked. Indian IT market will be more on partnership and risk sharing instead of standard consumption. Most of the large IT companies would gain in such a market while they may see a reversal in developed countries.

THE BEGINNING

Instead of penning a conclusion, we thought of putting the final thoughts, which in our view will be the beginning to the end of outsourcing era or beginning of Value Sourcing. Change is the only constant and everything what seems to be great today will be replaced with something more relevant sooner or later.

Having spent several years in our pursuit of excellence in technology management, it was clearly evident that technology is the only thing, which has made possible enablement of businesses and empowerment to customers like never before. We also believe that this is just a beginning and more possibilities that we can think of, may very soon become a reality for bringing value to whatever outsourcing is being done currently.

After Keith and myself created one of the most successful captive offshore development setup at Pune in India for Sears Holdings Corporation, we realized that the only difference between success and failure in this case was the willingness to change. Sears's team has been very forward looking and one of the most adaptable teams in accepting changes. What this team could bring out of their offshore location was unheard of by most of the similar setups for other companies. A setup, which was initially designed only for generating cost arbitrage grew up to generate intellectual properties and value way beyond original thoughts. The excellent team effort ended up creating the India setup as a high value-generating unit in just thirty months of its start.

Keith and myself have been thinking to share our experiences and experiments and created this first book together. It was very clear to us that there has to be something better than the outsourcing the world is experiencing today. It is however, not just left to the service provider to do everything, rather it is for the customer to demand for such value and keep looking for possibilities for better value beyond their standard outsourcing methods.

Our experiences and final results at Sears with the captive can be termed as one of such possibility that Sears looked three years back beyond their normal outsourcing. The result today can be termed nothing less than true "Value Sourcing" and this is just *the beginning.*

Acknowledgements

Idea of writing this book came to my mind more than a year back. Keith and myself always discussed on how we can plan out our activities in line with what will happen in future in the field of technology outsourcing. In essence, we were trying to decode the future based on the past history and started coming out with some answers on how the landscape of technology and its outsourcing will look like few years from now. It became even more important for us to decode the future because we were trying to build a great technology company, which is future ready and can lead the change in various areas, instead of getting challenged due to rapid transformation in technology and the way technology business will be conducted globally. The findings of our study and application of several of them in real life it became clear that future of IT outsourcing will be very different and even more challenging would be the fact that the huge population of technology talents may become outdated soon. The threat may not be just of up-skilling needs, but elimination of the complete outsourcing work as we see them today. For a vast majority, it might be a relearning exercise to adjust in the new paradigm.

Keith and myself were always wondering as to how come the real talents are becoming lesser and lesser in India where the world shops for technology today, but could see a lot of welcome initiatives for change too.

We would like to thank CIOs and senior technology and business leaders with whom we got great insights for this book, although we cannot put their name here.

Finally, I would like to thank my wife Nandani and son Manit for the great support in bearing with me several weekends and nights when I was busy completing this book.